EPISTLE TO THE HEBREWS

BIBLE GUIDES

The twenty-two volumes

1	THE MAKING OF THE BIBLE	*William Barclay*
2	IN THE BEGINNING	*Bernhard W. Anderson*
3	THE LAW GIVERS	*R. A. Barclay*
4	NATION MAKING	*Lawrence E. Toombs*
5	HISTORIANS OF ISRAEL (1)	*Gordon Robinson*
6	HISTORIANS OF ISRAEL (2)	*Hugh Anderson*
7	PROPHETS OF ISRAEL (1)	*George Knight*
8	PROPHETS OF ISRAEL (2)	*William Neil*
9	PROPHETS OF ISRAEL (3)	*John Mauchline*
10	SINGERS OF ISRAEL	*G. S. Gunn*
11	THE WISDOM OF ISRAEL	*John Paterson*
12	TRACTS FOR THE TIMES	*William McKane*
13	THE GOOD NEWS	*C. L. Mitton*
14	WORLD OF ST. JOHN	*E. Earle Ellis*
15	THE YOUNG CHURCH	*G. E. Ladd*
16	FREEDOM OF THE CHRISTIAN	*B. S. Mackay*
17	PAUL AND HIS CONVERTS	*F. F. Bruce*
18	LETTERS TO THE CHURCHES	*Morton S. Enslin*
19	EPISTLES FROM PRISON	*Donald Guthrie*
20	EPISTLE TO THE HEBREWS	*William Barclay*
21	GENERAL EPISTLES	*G. R. Beasley-Murray*
22	DREAMS OF THE FUTURE	*T. S. Kepler*

All the volumes have now been published.

BIBLE GUIDES

General Editors: William Barclay and F. F. Bruce

No. 20

EPISTLE TO
THE HEBREWS

by

WILLIAM BARCLAY

Professor of New Testament in the University of Glasgow

Published jointly by

LUTTERWORTH PRESS
LONDON

ABINGDON PRESS
NEW YORK AND NASHVILLE

First published 1965

ABBREVIATIONS

R.S.V. (Revised Standard Version of the Bible).
The Biblical quotations in this book are from the R.S.V.
A.V. (Authorized Version, King James Version of the Bible).
N.E.B. (New English Bible).

*Printed in Great Britain by
Cox & Wyman Ltd., London, Fakenham and Reading*

GENERAL INTRODUCTION

THE AIM of Bible Guides is to present in 22 volumes a total view of the Bible, and to present the purpose, plan and power of the Scriptures.

Bible Guides are free from the technicalities of Biblical scholarship but are soundly based on all the generally accepted conclusions of modern Bible research.

They are written in clear, simple, straightforward English. Each author has worked to a comprehensive editorial pattern so that the 22 volumes form a concise conspectus of the Bible.

THE AIM

The aim of Bible Guides is to offer a "guide" to the main themes of each book (or group of books) rather than a commentary on the text of the book. Through Bible Guides the Bible itself will speak its message, reveal its power and declare its purpose.

Bible Guides is essentially an undertaking for non-theologically equipped readers who want to know what the Bible is about, how its various parts came to be written and what their meaning is to-day. But the preacher, teacher, educator and expositor of all ranges of the Christian Church will find Bible Guides a series of books to buy and study. They combine the modern knowledge of the Bible together with all the evangelical zeal of sound Biblical expression—and all done in a handy readable compass.

EDITORIAL PLAN

In our suggestion to the writers of the various books we were careful to make the distinction between a "commentary" and a "guide". Our experience is that an adequate commentary on a book of the Bible requires adequate space and on the part of the student some equipment in the scholarly lore and technicalities of

Biblical research. A "guide", however, can be both selective and compressed and do what it sets out to do—guide the reader in an understanding of the book. That has been, and is, our aim.

As general editors we have had a good deal of experience among the various schools of Biblical interpretation. We are constantly surprised at the amount of common Biblical understanding which is acceptable to all types of Christian tradition and churchmanship. We hope that our Bible Guides reflect this and that they will be widely used, and welcomed as a contribution to Biblical knowledge and interpretation in the twentieth century.

THE WRITERS

The writers of Bible Guides represent a widely selected area of Biblical scholars, and all of them have co-operated enthusiastically in the editorial plan. They conceive their work to be that of examination, explanation and exposition of the book(s) of the Bible each is writing about. While they have worked loyally to the pattern we suggested they have been completely free in their presentation. Above all, they have remembered the present power and appeal of the Bible, and have tried to present its message and its authority for life to-day. In this sense Bible Guides is, we think, a fresh venture in the popular understanding of the Scriptures, combined as it is with the scholarly skill of our company of writers. We owe our thanks also to our publishers and their editors, Dr. Emory Stevens Bucke of the Abingdon Press of New York and Nashville, and Dr. Cecil Northcott of the Lutterworth Press of London. Their careful management and attention to publishing detail have given these Bible Guides a world wide constituency.

WILLIAM BARCLAY
F. F. BRUCE

CONTENTS

INTRODUCTION TO BIBLE GUIDES—THE EDITORS

AUTHOR'S FOREWORD

1. THE LETTER WHICH WOULD NOT BE DENIED   *Page* 11
Who is the writer?—Hebrews in history.

2. NAMING THE NAMELESS ONE   *Page* 22
The "orphan" letter—Did Paul have a hand?—Barnabas,
Stephen or Apollos—The Great Unknown.

3. IDENTIFYING THE DESTINATION   *Page* 35
The correspondents and their needs—Alexandria, Rome,
Ephesus—The traditional view—The Hebrews' loss and
gain—The priestly body.

4. IDENTIFYING THE FORM AND THE DATE   *Page* 51
Speech and not letter?—Homily or sermon?—Identifying
the date—A fixed point—The persecution of Nero—The
most likely date.

5. CHILD OF TWO WORLDS   *Page* 58
Jewish and Greek—Access to God through Christ.

6. THE SUPREMACY OF JESUS CHRIST   *Page* 63
The Splendour of Christ—The new priesthood—Christ's
lonely supremacy.

7. THE NEW AND GREATER PRIESTHOOD   *Page* 70
The order of Melchizedek—Christ's superior priesthood.

8. THE NEW RELATIONSHIP   *Page* 74

The Opener of the Way—The Covenant relationship—
Jesus, the mediator.

9. WORDS OF WARNING   *Page* 80

Characteristics of the message—Methods of interpretation—
Warnings of danger.

10. FAITH AND LIFE   *Page* 88

Faith, an intellectual conviction—Faith in life—Life in the
Church.

11. PERMANENT VALUES   *Page* 93

Access to God—The work of Christ—The seven dangers.

AUTHOR'S FOREWORD

My old chief G. H. C. Macgregor used to say that there was no book in the New Testament which produced such definite and opposite reactions in its readers as the Letter to the Hebrews does. You either found it, he used to say, one of the supreme books of the New Testament, or you found that it had little to say to you at all. Now it so happened that he himself was one of the people who felt that Hebrews had little to say to him; his whole mind and heart were steeped and saturated in his beloved Gospel of John; and because of this from the time I became his lecturer in 1947 it fell to me to lecture on Hebrews, both in the exegesis of its text and the exposition of its theology. It was fortunate that for me the Letter to the Hebrews was always one of the great products of the Christian faith, and the longer I studied it the more I loved it, and the greater it seemed to me.

It was, therefore, natural that when it came to the planning of this series I should wish to write the volume on the Letter to the Hebrews myself. And now I have done so. No one would call Hebrews an easy book to read; no one would say that it will yield its riches to the lazy reader who will not take the trouble necessary to understand it. But when we do study it it has riches to give. No book in the New Testament sets Jesus Christ more firmly in the centre of its teaching, and no book is more certain that Jesus Christ is the only way to God.

No doubt there are unacknowledged debts in this book, for when you have taught a book for many years, you have so assimilated what you have read about it that you lose the awareness of that which is your own and that which you have borrowed from other sources.

I have made frequent use of all the standard commentaries: Moffatt, Westcott, Wickham, Robinson, Narborough, Bruce, and the vast and indispensable French commentary of Spicq.

Hebrews has been fortunate in its expositors, Davidson, Dodds, Scott, Nairne, William Manson. The Introductions of Moffatt, McNeile, Clogg and Wikenhauser have been used. Reuss and Westcott on the Canon are invaluable for the canonical history of Hebrews, and Theron in *The Evidence of Tradition* assembled the patristic evidence.

I think that it may be that Hebrews is one of the neglected books of the New Testament except for a few great passages, and I hope that our journey through its history and thought together may help others to find it as precious as I have done.

University of Glasgow,
June, 1964

WILLIAM BARCLAY

THE LETTER WHICH WOULD NOT BE DENIED

IT WOULD BE true to say that the Letter to the Hebrews finally obtained a place in the New Testament because it could not be kept out. It was not without a struggle that it won its right to be part of the Scriptures. Its problem was this. No one knew who wrote it; it arrived on the scene like Melchizedek, without father or mother. At that time in the very earliest days the ultimate test of any book was whether or not it was the work of an apostle or at least of an apostolic man. If therefore a book was not the work of an apostle, it was not regarded as Scripture. So the position of the Letter to the Hebrews was that no one denied its spiritual greatness; no one denied that it was a book on which a man might feed his soul and enrich his mind and confirm his heart; no one denied that there were Churches in which for long it had been read and valued. But at the same time no one knew who the author was; and therefore it was not easy for it to become a part of the canon of the New Testament. But in the end the supreme value of the Letter made it impossible to keep it out, and the problem was solved by including it among the Letters of Paul, for Paul was the great letter-writer of the New Testament. Let us look at this story of the triumph of the Letter to the Hebrews, for in its own way it is a fascinating story.

There were up to the 4th century three attitudes to the Letter to the Hebrews in the early Church and among its scholars. First, there was the attitude which connected Hebrews with Paul, but not directly. This attitude held that Hebrews, as it stands, is not the work of Paul, but that it has a more or less close connection with him. The second attitude did not connect Hebrews with Paul at all, and equally did not connect it with any other writer. This attitude regarded Hebrews as anonymous —the work of an unknown author. The third attitude attributed

Hebrews to some other author altogether. And these three attitudes were represented in the traditions of three great sections of the ancient Church.

The first attitude was the attitude of the Church at Alexandria. Alexandria was the great centre of Biblical scholarship in the ancient Church. The famous catechetical school at Alexandria had in charge of it a series of outstanding Christian Biblical scholars. The first of them was Pantaenus (about A.D. 200). He observed two things about Hebrews. First, he observed that the tradition that he had received connected it with Paul; second, he observed that, as he knew it, the title of the Letter was simply *The Letter to the Hebrews* with no author's name mentioned at all. His explanation was that Paul had written it. But in humility Paul had not put his name to it, because the apostle to the Hebrews was none other than Jesus Himself (3 : 1). Paul was the apostle to the Gentiles, and with that title he was well content and he would never have dared to take his Lord's title. So Paul wrote the Letter, as it were, as an extra and never put his name to it at all. This is the judgment of Pantaenus which Clement his successor hands down (Eusebius, *The Ecclesiastical History* 6 . 14).

Clement himself (about A.D. 215) took the matter a little further. The Alexandrians were great Greek scholars; Clement himself had an astonishing knowledge of Greek literature. Now to anyone who knew Greek it was clear that the Greek style of Hebrews is quite different from that of Paul, so different that it was not really possible to think that Paul wrote it as it stands. Clement formed the opinion that the style of Hebrews is very like that of Acts; so he came to the conclusion that Paul had written the Letter in Hebrew to the Jews, and that Luke had carefully and lovingly translated it into Greek and had so made it available for the Greeks. Clement explained the fact that Paul's name did not appear in the title of the Letter by suggesting that the Jews were suspicious of Paul, and would have approached anything he wrote with a prejudice against it; so Paul omitted his own name in the title so that the Jews would not be initially repelled from reading the Letter (Eusebius, *The Ecclesiastical History* 6 . 14).

Clement's successor in Alexandria was Origen (about A.D.255), and he was the greatest scholar of them all. He said that Paul could not actually have written the Letter, because the style is not Paul's. It is, he says, much more "Greek" than Paul's style, and it is true that the author of the Letter to the Hebrews writes Greek that is almost classical in its purity and that is consistently the best in the New Testament. He goes on to say that he thinks that the thought is the thought of Paul, and that the Letter was written by someone who had made notes of and remembered Paul's teaching and who had then set it down in his own words and language. He therefore says that if any Church chooses to hold that the Letter is Paul's they are not to be blamed, for they have tradition on their side, and the thought is substantially that of Paul. He then went on to make his famous statement: "But who wrote the Letter God only knows for certain." He then mentions reports that he has heard that Clement of Rome or Luke had written the Letter. "On this," he says, "I will say no more" (Eusebius, *The Ecclesiastical History* 6 . 25). He himself habitually quoted the Letter as Paul's, and he was quite prepared to undertake to prove that it was thoroughly Pauline in thought in answer to those who wished to reject it altogether because it was not actually written by Paul (*Letter to Africanus* 9). Origen had no doubt of the value of the Letter; he had no trouble in believing that the mind of Paul could be seen in it; but for him the actual author was the great unknown.

The next of the great Greek scholars at whose judgment we must look is Eusebius (about A.D. 340) whose *Ecclesiastical History* we have already more than once quoted. Eusebius was one of the first Christian scholars to make a deliberate study of what books were universally accepted in the Church and what books were in doubt, or actually rejected. The strange position of Hebrews is seen from the fact that at one time he includes it among the books which are universally accepted, and at another amongst those about which there is argument. He himself accepted it and said he thought that Paul had written it in Hebrew and that Clement of Rome had translated it. He tells us that some did not accept it, because the Roman Church did not accept it as

Paul's. His own point of view was that the Letter already had such a long and honourable record in the Church that it was entirely reasonable to include it among the great apostle's writings (*The Ecclesiastical History* 3 . 25 ; 6 . 13 ; 3 . 3 ; 3 . 38). The point of view of Eusebius was that Hebrews was of such value that he could do no other than accept it.

We come now to the end of the story in the Alexandrian and the Greek-speaking Church. The situation is that the great Alexandrians knew and used and loved Hebrews; they also knew that as it stood it could not be the work of Paul, for its Greek is not Paul's Greek, and indeed its thought is not always Paul's thought. They tried in one way or another to connect it with Paul; but Pauline or not the Letter was so great and vital that they never even dreamed of rejecting it.

The matter was finally settled in A.D. 367. In that year the great champion of Christian orthodoxy Athanasius wrote his famous Easter Letter to his people. He knew that there were many heretics in the Church; he knew that strange and disturbing and mistaken books were circulating; and so he listed in his Letter the books which are "canonical and divine". And for the first time the list is exactly that of our New Testament, and Hebrews is unquestioningly included as one of the fourteen Letters of Paul. As far as the Alexandrian Church was concerned, once and for all Hebrews has become part of the New Testament, and its place has been assured by bringing it under the wing of Paul. The only way to make certain that this great Letter could secure its place was to list it among the works of the Church's great letter-writer. The Alexandrians knew that Hebrews was not Pauline; but they wanted above all things to keep it, and they saw that it was great enough to attribute to Paul, and so they listed it among his Letters, and Hebrews' place in the New Testament was finally safe.

We now turn to the Churches of the West, and in particular to the attitude of the Church at Rome. In this area Hebrews had a still harder struggle, for these Churches did not regard the Letter as even indirectly connected with Paul; they regarded it as anonymous, a Letter whose author was unknown, and which therefore could not have canonical and scriptural authority. It was not that they did not value it, and it was not that many of them did not use it and quote it. It was rather that Hebrews held a kind of intermediate position. It was not fully Scripture; and yet it was not simply an "ordinary" book; it had to wait for more than two hundred years for the influence of a great scholar and churchman finally to authenticate it. Let us look at the story.

Hebrews emerged into the light of day in the West before it did in the East. About A.D. 95 there was a Clement who was Bishop of Rome; just as in the days of Paul, so in his day there was trouble in Corinth and Clement wrote to try to clear up the situation; and in his Letter to the Church at Corinth he quotes Hebrews extensively, unmistakably and at length. But he never mentions the author of it, and, if he had believed it to be Paul's, it is quite certain that he would have quoted it as such, especially in writing to one of Paul's own Churches. So in the West as early as the end of the 1st century Hebrews is used and known and valued, but even by that time the name of its author was lost.

For the next three centuries there is little to say about Hebrews in the West, although that little is significant and important. Justin Martyr (about A.D. 150) does not ever quote Hebrews by name, but he does use the title "Apostle" of Jesus, which is found in Hebrews only (Hebrews 3 : 1), and he does use Psalm 110 about Jesus, which is characteristic of Hebrews (Justin, *Apology* 1 . 12, 63 ; *Dialogue with Trypho* 96, 113). He seems to have known the thought and the ideas of Hebrews, but not to have regarded it as Scripture. Irenaeus (about 200), the Church's great exposer of heresies, in his *Against Heresies* quotes every Pauline Letter except Philemon, but never at any time quotes Hebrews, and, if he had regarded Hebrews as Scripture, he would quite certainly have used it in his defence of the faith.

But the most significant thing of all happened towards the end of the 2nd century. At this time the Church at Rome was forced to define the books which it regarded as the books of the faith; it had to do this in answer to the heretics who introduced their own books and who accepted and rejected the Church's books as they liked, and as suited their own erroneous beliefs. It was then that for the first time the Church drew up an official list of the books which constituted the New Testament. This very important document is known as the Muratorian Canon, after the scholar Muratori who discovered it. It lists the books and it briefly describes each one of them. There is no mention of Hebrews. Paul, it is said, wrote thirteen Letters to seven Churches and to three individuals. It enumerates them and describes them, and Hebrews is not one of them. At that time the official view was that Hebrews was not Pauline and was not scriptural or canonical.

Who is the Writer?

And now we come to the great Latin scholar whose influence finally tipped the scales in favour of Hebrews. His name was Jerome (about A.D. 400), and Jerome's place in Christian Biblical scholarship is for ever safe, for it was Jerome who produced the Latin Vulgate. The interesting thing about Jerome is that from his writings we can trace his developing attitude to Hebrews over a period of fourteen years. In A.D. 392 he writes (*Concerning Famous Men* 59) that Gaius of Rome had counted only thirteen Letters of Paul, and had said that the fourteenth, the one entitled the Letter to the Hebrews, is not his. He then goes on to say: "To this day it is not regarded as Paul's by the Romans." He then proceeds to tell what the Alexandrians had said about Hebrews and about its indirect connection with Paul. In A.D. 394 in a letter to Paulina (*Letter* 53 . 8) he outlines the contents of the New Testament, and then goes on to say: "The Apostle Paul wrote to seven Churches; the eighth Letter, the Letter to the Hebrews, is by many regarded as not to be included in the list."

In his commentaries he frequently cites the Letter to the Hebrews, but his method of citation shows his own uncertainty. He cites it as follows: "Whoever it is who wrote the Letter to the Hebrews" (*On Amos* 3 . 8); "Paul the Apostle in the Letter to the Hebrews which the Latin custom does not accept" (*On*

Isaiah 3 . 6); "Paul the Apostle says, that is, if you accept the Letter to the Hebrews" (*On Exodus* 9 . 28); "Paul in the Letter which he wrote to the Hebrews, although many of the Latins regard it as doubtful" (*On Matthew* 4 . 26). It is quite clear that Jerome himself was more and more content to accept Hebrews, although he was quite aware that there was a large body of opinion which did not. But finally in a letter to Dardanus (*Letter* 129 . 3) in A.D. 414 he set down his own view in full:

"It must be said that this Letter which is addressed to the Hebrews has been accepted as Paul's not only by the Churches of the East but also by all the later Greek-speaking writers of the Church, although there are many who attribute it either to Barnabas or to Clement. It makes no difference whose it is, since they are all men of the Church, and since to-day it is frequently read in the Church. If the custom of the Latins does not receive it as included among the canonical Scriptures, neither do the Greek Churches with the same liberty accept the Revelation of John. As for ourselves we accept both, for we do not follow the custom of the present day but the authority of the ancient writers, who very commonly made abundant quotations from both, and that not as they occasionally cite the books of the Apocryphal Scriptures—or as they very rarely cite illustrations from heathen literature—but as canonical books of the Church." Here is the decision. For Jerome it is true that there were still many for whom Hebrews was in doubt, but the testimony of the Church, the witness of the fathers, the continued spiritual value of Hebrews left him in no doubt that Hebrews was Scripture, and he was content to include it with the Letters of Paul.

It is quite true that doubts lingered on. Hilary and Pelagius in their commentaries comment on only thirteen Letters of Paul, but now as in the East so in the West Hebrews has won its battle and is in the New Testament. It might not be possible to prove that it was Paul's; it was impossible to deny that it was the word of God, whoever wrote it.

We come now to the last attitude to the Letter to the Hebrews, the attitude which did not even indirectly attach it to the name of Paul, but which attributed it to some other author altogether.

We find this attitude in North Africa. Tertullian in his rigorist frame of mind was insisting on the seriousness of adultery and fornication and on the fact that they constituted mortal sin. To support this view he had evidence in Hebrews 6 which lays it down that there can be no forgiveness for deliberate apostasy and sin after baptism. So then he introduces this passage from Hebrews. He does so by saying that he is going to introduce certain evidence as an extra, the evidence of one who was a particular comrade of the apostles. He then goes on to say: "There is extant a Letter to the Hebrews under the name of Barnabas," which, he continues, "is more generally received among the Churches than the Shepherd of Hermas." So then in North Africa in the latter half of the 3rd century Hebrews was not regarded as a letter of Paul's at all, and it was not even regarded as Scripture. And it was regarded as the work of Barnabas.

In North Africa at this time Hebrews was not part of the New Testament at all. Cyprian (about A.D. 250) never quotes it. Here also Hebrews had the same struggle for recognition as it had in other spheres of the Church. Slowly it gained ground; but even when it was generally accepted there was still a kind of question mark against it. The Synod of Carthage in A.D. 397 listed the books which are to be regarded as Divine Scripture. In regard to this matter its verdict runs: "The thirteen Letters of the Apostle Paul, and of the same author one Letter to the Hebrews." Still Hebrews stands in a kind of detachment from the other Letters.

As in the other spheres of the Church so in North Africa the influence of one man was decisive and in this case the man was Augustine (about 400 A.D.). Augustine was well aware of the doubts and the questionings and to some extent at least he shared them. He speaks of the Letter to the Hebrews, "which many declare to be Paul's, but which some indeed deny" (*The City of God* 16 . 22). In his Exposition of Romans II he says that it differs from all the other generally accepted Letters of Paul in that it has no salutation, in that it presents itself as anonymous, and in that it has no mention of the author's name. For this reason "some have feared to receive it into the canon of Scripture". In his work *On Forgiveness* (1 . 27, 50) he says that some have their doubts about Hebrews but with him the fact that the Eastern Churches have it in their canon of Scripture outweighs the doubts. And finally in his work *Concerning Christian Doctrine* (2 . 8, 12) he specifically and definitely includes it in the canon of Scripture.

Once again the Letter to the Hebrews arrived in the New Testament because it could not be kept out, and because a great leader of the Church found its undoubted claims to inspiration weightier than all the doubts as to its origin.

It is an odd fact that even in certain of the great Greek manuscripts the doubt about Hebrews is reflected. In Codex Claromontanus there is a list of New Testament books, and Hebrews is apparently listed in it as the Letter of Barnabas. Many of the later manuscripts are bilingual, that is to say they are written in both Latin and Greek with the Greek on one side of the page and the Latin translation on the other. In two 9th century manuscripts, Codex Augiensis and Codex Boernerianus, Hebrews is the only book to be only in Latin with no Greek at all. One of the most important manuscript discoveries for many years was the discovery of the Chester Beatty papyri in 1933, and in the manuscript which contains the Pauline Letters and Hebrews it has been noted that the text of Hebrews is much better than the text of the other Letters; and the deduction is that before it was incorporated into the manuscript Hebrews must have been copied separately and independently, apart from all the others.

Hebrews in History

For many centuries in the Middle Ages scholarship was rare and almost dead, but with the Renaissance and the Reformation Biblical scholarship flowered again, and once again Hebrews came often under question and sometimes under fire. Calvin never doubted the inspiration of Hebrews, but he did seriously doubt and even deny that Paul wrote it. He writes: "I embrace the Letter to the Hebrews without doubt among the Apostolic

Epistles; nor do I doubt that it was through a device of Satan that some have questioned its authority . . . Wherefore let us not allow the Church of God and ourselves to be bereft of so great a blessing; but let us vindicate for ourselves the possession of it with firmness. We need however feel little anxiety as to who wrote it . . . I cannot myself be brought to believe that Paul was the author . . . The method of instruction and style show that the writer was not Paul."

Luther went much further. For Luther, as Westcott says, there was a gospel within the gospel, a New Testament within the New Testament. "Briefly St. John's Gospel and his First Epistle, St. Paul's Epistles, specially those to the Romans, Galatians, Ephesians, and St. Peter's first Epistle; these are the books which shew thee Christ, and teach all which is needful and blessed for thee to know, even if you never see or hear any other book, or any other doctrine." Luther therefore went the length of placing four books in a group apart from "the true and certain Capital-books of the New Testament". These four books, placed at the end of his New Testament and not numbered, were Hebrews, James, Jude and the Revelation. To him these were definitely secondary books. So he says that Hebrews was quite certainly written not by an apostle, but by one of the disciples of the apostles. It is "put together out of many pieces". The writer "does not lay the foundation of faith, but yet he builds upon it gold, silver, precious stones. Therefore even if we find perhaps wood, straw, or hay, mingled with it, that shall not prevent us from receiving such instruction with all honour; though we do not place it absolutely on the same footing as the Apostolic Epistles." Luther quite definitely and openly gives Hebrews a secondary place.

The position of Erasmus is most interesting of all, and it is worth recounting because it shows very well the position of the Roman Catholic Church in regard to Biblical scholarship at the time of the Reformation. Erasmus was a great scholar and he well knew the early uncertainties about Hebrews and he was well aware that the Greek was not the Greek of Paul. Nonetheless he never doubted the apostolic inspiration of the Letter. It might not be Paul's, but it was "intensely close to the spirit and the heart of Paul". He is however astonished that anyone should claim any kind of certainty about its authorship. If however the Church definitely insists that it is Pauline "I am perfectly willing to subject my intellect to the demands of faith". He is quite clear in his own mind that the Letter is not Paul's, but he does not think that the matter is worth arguing about.

But in 1527 the official wrath descended on Erasmus' head. He was accused of arrogance and schism in that by denying the Pauline authorship he had denied the opinions of all the doctors of the Church and all the Councils of the Church. In his pride and pertinacity he had made himself wiser than the whole world. Whereupon Erasmus made an astonishing statement. "From the point of view of human intellect," he said, "I do not believe that this letter is Paul's . . . I could assemble many arguments to prove this. But it is more important to avoid causing the slightest stumbling-block to the weak. For with me the expressed judgment of the Church has more weight than all human reasonings." His one doubt is as to whether the Church insists that titles of the New Testament books are to be accepted as being as inspired as their contents. But whatever his own opinion he will accept what the Church chooses to say about them. "Without difficulty I subject my mind to the Church's authority, not only in this, but in all other matters." Erasmus the scholar was under the necessity of committing intellectual suicide to remain Erasmus the churchman.

It is unnecessary to carry the story further. In every part of the Church the Letter to the Hebrews had a battle to fight; its handicap was that it was the product of the mind and the heart of some great unknown. But such was its power over the minds and the hearts of men that nothing could debar it from its rightful place in Scripture, and, even although they knew that it was not his at least directly, men rightly felt that they did Paul no wrong by putting it under his protection and by ensuring its inclusion in the New Testament by attaching it to his name.

2

NAMING THE NAMELESS ONE

WE HAVE SEEN that almost from the moment it emerges in Christian history and literature the Letter to the Hebrews was an orphan letter without parentage, and with a nameless author. We have also seen that to ensure its entry into the canon of Scripture it had to be put under the protection of the name of Paul, the greatest of the letter-writers. But from the earliest days until now the greatest Biblical scholars have been sure that however great Hebrews is, and however worthy it is to be ascribed to him, the letter was not written by Paul. That conclusion has been reached on two grounds.

The 'Orphan' Letter

i. The style is not the style of Paul. This is what impressed Origen long ago. "The verbal style of the Letter to the Hebrews," he said, "is not unskilled (the word he uses means rather *unprofessional*) like the language of the apostle who acknowledged himself to be 'unskilled in speech' (2 Corinthians 11 : 6), that is, in expression." He goes on: "That its diction is purer Greek (literally, more Greek Greek) anyone who has power to discern differences in phraseology will acknowledge" (Eusebius, *The Ecclesiastical History* 6 . 25 . 11). The Greek of Hebrews is the Greek of the expert professional; the Greek of Paul's letters is the Greek of the technically untrained layman. Even in an English translation it is easy to see that the style of Hebrews is much more smooth and serene and polished than the vivid, rugged, tempestuous style of Paul. Paul's excited language flows like a cataract and a torrent; he pours out his rebuke, his praise, his exposition like a pastor who does not much care how he says a thing so long as the thing is understood; the writer to the Hebrews writes more like an orator polishing and adorning his sentences and choosing his words with almost as much care as he chose his thought. This is the kind of difference in style which really does indicate difference in authorship, for it springs not so much from a difference in training, as from a difference in temperament and personality. The two styles are not the styles of the same man writing at different times; the two styles are the styles of two different men.

ii. If the style is different, the thought is even more fundamentally different. To Paul Judaism and Christianity are over against each other. Judaism is the Law, and the Law is an evil force from which a man must wrench himself free; the Law is the flat contradiction of Christianity and of grace. For the writer to the Hebrews Christianity much more definitely grows out of Judaism. The Law and all the ordinances and rituals of Judaism are not in themselves in any way bad; they are rather types, shadows, outlines, images of that which was to come. For him Christianity is much more the fulfilment of Judaism. The Law and all the ceremonies and rituals are not so much contradictions as they are foreshadowings of Christ and Christianity.

For the writer to the Hebrews Christianity is not so much something which is contradictory of Judaism as it is something which is better than Judaism. The number of times that the word *better* occurs in his Letter is very significant. For the Christian a better hope is introduced (7 : 19). Jesus is the surety of a better covenant (7 : 22). Christ has obtained a ministry which is much more excellent than the old (8 : 6). Christ is the minister of a greater and more perfect tabernacle (9 : 11). For the Christian there are better sacrifices (9 : 23). The Christian has better promises (8 : 6). It is not the opposition and the contradiction that the writer to the Hebrews stresses; it is the betterness, the superiority, the fact that the readers of the Letter ought to have passed through the one and come to the other.

The attitude of the writer to the Hebrews to Judaism differs radically from that of Paul; and this may well be so because Paul and the writer to the Hebrews had quite

23

different ideas about what Judaism is. To Paul Judaism was basically a legal system which aimed at obtaining merit in the sight of God; to the writer to the Hebrews Judaism was basically a sacrificial system which sought to enable men to approach God. It is true that neither these nor any human sacrifice could open the way to God, but they were not so much wrong as foreshadowings of the perfect sacrifice which was to come in Jesus Christ. For Paul on the other hand the Law was positively wrong. Paul saw Judaism as the contradiction of Christianity; the writer to the Hebrews saw it as the foreshadowing of Christianity. Paul saw Judaism as something wrong; the writer to the Hebrews saw Judaism as something inadequate. Paul looks at Judaism from the point of view of the Law; the writer to the Hebrews looks at Judaism from the point of view of sacrifice. Paul looked on Judaism as an ethical system designed to acquire merit; the writer to the Hebrews looked at Judaism as a sacrificial system designed to enable men to approach the presence of God. We may put it in this way: Paul looked at Judaism from the standpoint of the Rabbi and the Synagogue; the writer to the Hebrews looked at Judaism from the standpoint of the Priest and the Temple. The result is that for Paul Judaism is wrong and misguided, while for the writer to the Hebrews it is only imperfect and inadequate.

Apart from many lesser details of difference there is one difference which can be recognized just as easily in the English as in the Greek. Paul's favourite way of speaking of Jesus is to call him Our Lord Jesus Christ, or Christ Jesus our Lord. In his Letters these two forms of address occur between them almost seventy times; but the writer to the Hebrews refers to Jesus simply as Jesus, as the Lord or our Lord, as Christ. Only once does he speak of our Lord Jesus, and Paul's characteristic way of speaking of Christ Jesus never occurs in Hebrews at all.

It is clear that there is a different mind behind both the style and the thought of Hebrews and the Letters of Paul.

There is one simple fact which would quite certainly rule out the Pauline authorship of Hebrews. Very early in the Letter the writer speaks both of himself and of those to whom he writes and of the way in which the Gospel came to them, and of the salvation which they have received. "It was declared at first by the Lord, and it was attested to us by those who heard him" (2 : 3). Here the writer quite definitely sets himself and his readers among the Christians who received the message of the Gospel, not direct from Jesus Christ, but from the apostles. Christ gave the message to the apostles; the apostles transmitted it to them. Of all things, this is the one thing Paul would never have said. His whole claim and glory was that his experience of Jesus Christ was absolutely direct and at first hand and with no one between. Paul would never have called himself a second generation Christian, and that is what both the writer and the readers of the Letter to the Hebrews were. Paul would never for one moment have agreed that he had got his Christianity at second hand. Apart from all the other arguments, this one argument alone would prove that Hebrews as it stands is certainly not from the pen of Paul.

Did Paul Have a Hand?

Before we look at some of the people who have been suggested as authors of this Letter, we must first look at the suggestion which seeks to connect it indirectly with Paul, the suggestion that he wrote it in Hebrew and that it was translated into Greek. Two of the great early Christian scholars noted this suggestion with approval. Clement of Alexandria said that Paul wrote it in Hebrew for the Hebrews, and that Luke carefully translated it and published it for the Greeks (Eusebius, *The Ecclesiastical History* 6 . 14 . 2). Jerome says that there is a suggestion that Paul wrote most fluently in Hebrew, which was his own tongue, and that that which he said eloquently in Hebrew was turned into still more eloquent Greek. He suggests that either Luke or Clement of Rome did the translating, and that, he says, is why this Letter differs from all the others (*Concerning Famous Men* 5).

What is there to be said for this suggestion? In the first place, it is true to say that no Letter ever read less like a translation than the Letter to the Hebrews does. Its Greek is real Greek, written by a man who spoke Greek, and not translation Greek. In the second place, when the writer to the Hebrews quotes the Old Testament, it is not the Hebrew Old Testament that he quotes, but the Septuagint, the Greek Old Testament, and sometimes his points are such that it is from the Greek Old Testament and not the Hebrew Old Testament that he is making them. It is from the Greek and not from the Hebrew that he starts. In the third place, he is fond of alliteration and of plays on words, and these cannot be transferred from one language to another. No one can translate a pun or an alliteration from one language to another. In the fourth place, there is one definite example of this which in Hebrew would be impossible. The writer to the Hebrews talks much about the old and the new *covenant*. In Greek the word for covenant is *diathēkē*; now it so happens that *diathēkē* is also the regular word for a will. Of course, a will does not become operative until the death of the testator. And the new covenant did not become operative until the death of Jesus Christ. The writer to the Hebrews plays on the double meaning of *diathēkē*; he so to speak puns on the word. The passage is in 9 : 15, 16 :

> Therefore he is the mediator of a new covenant, so that those who are called may receive the promised eternal inheritance, since a death has occurred which redeems them from the transgressions under the first *covenant*. For where a *will* is involved, the death of the one who made it must be established.

As the R.S.V. notes, the word for *covenant* and the word for *will* is the same word in Greek, the word *diathēkē*; it is a play on words, and it could not be reproduced in Hebrew at all, for the Hebrew word for *covenant*, *berith*, cannot mean *will* at all. This cannot be translation; this could only have been written in Greek.

We can be quite certain that the Letter to the Hebrews is not a translation from Hebrew; it was written in Greek from the very beginning. It is therefore not possible to say that someone translated into Greek that which Paul had written in Hebrew. This theory will not do.

If then we have to agree that Paul could not have been directly the writer of Hebrews, and if we have to reject as untenable the suggestion that Hebrews is a Greek translation of something that Paul wrote in Hebrew or in Aramaic, we must go on to pass in review some of the suggestions which have been made about possible authors for this letter. It is natural to look first at the three names with which Hebrews was actually connected in the speculations of the early Church. Both Clement of Alexandria and Origen mention the possibility that Luke may have had something to do with Hebrews either as writer or translator, and Origen further adds the suggestion that Clement of Rome was connected with it. Jerome records the suggestion that either Clement of Rome or Luke may be involved, and also reminds us that Tertullian attributed Hebrews to Barnabas (Eusebius, *The Ecclesiastical History* 6 . 14 . 2-4 ; 6 . 25 . 11-14 ; Jerome, *Concerning Famous Men* 5 ; Tertullian, *On Modesty* 20). It is as well to begin with the suggestions for which there is some kind of evidence, even if the evidence is uncertain, hazy and nebulous.

i. First then Luke is suggested as an author for Hebrews. Luke was certainly at the centre of Christian activity in the early Church. He was of all men most faithful to Paul (2 Timothy 4 : 11). He was one of those men who got his Christianity not direct from Jesus Christ but from the apostles (Hebrews 2 : 3). He is the author of Luke and of Acts. And he does, like the writer to the Hebrews, write excellent Greek, the Greek of one whose native tongue is Greek.

But there is too much to be said on the other side. No doubt Luke's Greek is good, but it has not the oratorical cast of that of the writer to the Hebrews. Hebrews is an essay in what we might call speculative theology; the writer to the Hebrews was one of the great theological thinkers of the New Testament. There is no sign at all that Luke's gifts lay that way. He was an historian and had the gift of pictorial and vivid writing, but he was not a theologian. And is it likely that a Greek convert, perhaps first to Judaism and then to Christianity, would have such a scholarly and detailed knowledge of the Old Testament and of the Tabernacle and of the priestly and the sacrificial system?

There is no real reason for thinking that Luke could have written, or did write, Hebrews.

ii. Second, there is Clement of Rome. Undoubtedly Clement knew Hebrews and undoubtedly he quotes it. But there are three things to be said. First, anyone who has read Clement's Letter to the Corinthians will agree that he had a pedestrian and second-rate mind. He was an earnest and good man, but on the evidence of the Letter he certainly did write, he simply did not possess the intellectual powers to write the Letter to the Hebrews. Second, Clement was Bishop of Rome. Now later on the Roman Church rejected the Letter to the Hebrews, because they did not know who had written it. Surely if the Bishop of Rome had written the Letter to the Hebrews, the Church at Rome would have known that he had. If Clement of Rome had written Hebrews, the Church at Rome would never have been in a position to say that its author was unknown to them. Third, Clement lived and worked at the very end of the 1st century. If he wrote Hebrews, it could only have been somewhere between A.D. 90 and 100; and, as we shall see, that is almost certainly much too late a date for the Letter. There is little likelihood that Clement of Rome had anything to do with the writing of Hebrews however well he knew it and however much he valued it and used it.

Barnabas, Stephen or Apollos

iii. There is Barnabas. It may well be that the claims of Barnabas must be taken seriously; for he is the one person, other than Paul, to whom the Letter was in so many words attributed. Tertullian seems definitely to have regarded it as his.

Barnabas is an obvious candidate; he is in fact in many ways the most obvious candidate of all. He was at one time the fellow-worker of Paul; he was an apostolic man; he was clearly known and trusted in the Church of Jerusalem, for it was he who sponsored Paul (Acts 9 : 27). The name Barnabas means a son of consolation (Acts 4 : 36), and the Letter to the Hebrews calls

28

itself a word of consolation (13 : 22). Barnabas being a native of Cyprus would be a native Greek speaker, and above all Barnabas was a Levite and therefore thoroughly familiar with the function of the priesthood and with the Temple sacrificial ritual.

But there is something to be said on the other side. Barnabas, as we find him pictured in Acts, gives no indication that he is of the mental calibre of the man who wrote the Letter to the Hebrews. And further there is this to be said. It is quite clear that Barnabas' knowledge of the Temple and the ritual must have been first hand, because he was actually a Levite. But on the other hand it is quite clear that the knowledge of the writer to the Hebrews was not first hand; it is scholarly, academic and archaeological. Two things stand out about his knowledge of the priestly and sacrificial ritual. It is not the Jerusalem Temple that he is talking about at all, but the Tabernacle in the wilderness. It is from the ancient Tabernacle, not the contemporary Temple, that he draws his types and his symbols and his imagery. And, what is more, there are at least two occasions when he is in error. The High Priests did not, as he says they did, make daily sacrifice for their own sins; they did that only on the Day of Atonement (7 : 27); and the golden altar of the incense was not in the Holy of Holies, nor were the golden pot of manna and Aaron's rod that budded in the ark of the covenant (9 : 3, 4). The writer to the Hebrews has an academic knowledge of the Tabernacle, and even there he can slip up; this could not be true of Barnabas whose work once lay in the Temple.

Attractive as the case for Barnabas may look at first sight, it does not bear closer examination.

When we pass beyond the names of Luke, Clement of Rome and Barnabas we enter into the realm of speculation, and some of the guesses at the author's name are very interesting and even very attractive. Let us look at some of them.

i. It has been suggested that Stephen wrote Hebrews. The argument is that there are several significant resemblances between the speech of Stephen (Acts 7 : 2-53) and the thought and language of Hebrews. Stephen's review of history is not unlike the review of the writer to the Hebrews in Hebrews 11.

Abraham, Moses, Joshua and the building of the Temple appear in both. Both Stephen and Hebrews talk of the Tabernacle being built according to the pattern which was shown to Moses by God (Acts 7 : 44 ; Hebrews 8 : 5). In the early stories the Law is given direct by the hands of God into the hands of Moses. Later Judaism became obsessed with the idea of the transcendence of God, the majesty of God, and therefore the immense and unbridgeable distance between God and man, and the impossibility of God ever dealing as it were face to face and directly with men. Later Judaism therefore introduced the idea of angels, and spoke of the Law as being given to Moses not directly by the hands of God but through angels as intermediaries. In both the speech of Stephen and the Letter to the Hebrews it is through angels that the Law comes (Acts 7 : 38 ; Hebrews 2 : 2). Above all, right through Stephen's speech there runs the idea that Christianity is the consummation and the complete development of Judaism, that, so to speak, the evolution of Judaism finds its summit and its peak and its divine fulfilment in Jesus Christ and in the Christian gospel. And with this there goes the closely inter-related conviction that, if Judaism fails to accept Christ and Christianity, it has refused its own destiny and its own fulfilment, and can hope for nothing but condemnation and extinction. This is very close indeed to the conception of Hebrews that Judaism was a shadow and outline and foretaste of the greater things that were to come with Christ. Further, Stephen's conviction that the time of ancient sacrifice is gone, and that the approach to God is not via the Temple ritual but is open to all, is very close to the basic thought of Hebrews.

It can be seen that there are very close resemblances between the thought of Stephen and the thought of Hebrews, but it is hardly the case that the resemblances are so close that the case is proved, and the argument that Stephen wrote it demands so early a date for Hebrews that the connection is hardly possible.

ii. Hebrews has been connected with another of the Seven (Acts 6 : 5). It has been connected with Philip. We know that Philip stayed at Caesarea and we know that Paul for some time stayed with him (Acts 21 : 8). It is only natural to think that during his two years' imprisonment in Caesarea Paul would see a great deal of Philip, and that they would talk much together. It is suggested that, when James the head of the Jerusalem Church died a martyr's death, there was a split in the Church, and that the more Jewish section of the Church, rid of the mediating influence of James, wished to turn completely away from Paul and to relapse again into their ancestral Judaism, and so to make Christianity a thing of the Temple and the Law. It is then suggested that just at that time Philip wrote the Letter to the Hebrews to warn them against the danger of relapsing into Judaism, that he wrote it in complete consultation and collaboration with Paul, and that Paul actually added the verses in 13 : 22-25 to attest the Letter.

That reconstruction is reasonable enough. No doubt Philip was a very important figure in the early Church, for he was in fact the Church's first foreign missionary (Acts 8). But it is the kind of theory which can neither be proved nor disproved, and Philip was so considerable a figure in the Church that it is difficult to see how his name went lost, if he really did write the Letter. If under these circumstances Philip did write Hebrews, it is difficult to see how some tradition of his authorship did not linger in the Jerusalem Church.

iii. Hebrews has been attributed to Peter. A letter to the Hebrews might well be thought to be Peter's, for he was the apostle who was distinctively entrusted with the mission to the circumcision (Galatians 2 : 7). Apart from that general consideration, it is claimed that there are a number of very suggestive resemblances between Peter's first Letter and the Letter to the Hebrews.

Both Letters speak of Christians as strangers, aliens and pilgrims in this world (Hebrews 11 : 13 ; 1 Peter 2 : 11). Both Letters liken the Church to a house and a household (Hebrews 3 : 6 ; 10 : 21 ; 1 Peter 2 : 5 ; 4 : 17). Both Letters speak of the living word of God (Hebrews 4 : 12 ; 1 Peter 1 : 23). Both Letters speak of Jesus as the Shepherd of His people (Hebrews 13 : 20 ; 1 Peter 2 : 25). Both Letters speak of Jesus bearing sin (*anenegkein hamartias*) (Hebrews 9 : 28 ; 1 Peter 2 : 24). Both Letters use the word *amōmos*, spotless, without blemish, of Jesus

(Hebrews 9 : 14 ; 1 Peter 1 : 19). Both Letters speak of the Christians being persecuted for the reproach of the name of Jesus Christ (Hebrews 11 : 26 ; 13 : 13 ; 1 Peter 4 : 14). Both Letters speak of themselves as a brief exhortation (Hebrews 13 : 22 ; 1 Peter 5 : 12). Both Letters pronounce a very similar blessing (Hebrews 13 : 21 ; 1 Peter 5 : 10).

It is undoubtedly possible to build up an impressive list of resemblances between First Peter and Hebrews. But identity of authorship produces one insoluble problem. If Hebrews is Peter's, why is there not the slightest tradition to connect it with him? Peter was the premier apostle and, if he did write Hebrews, it is difficult if not impossible to understand why his name is never in tradition connected with it.

One would have thought that the statement that the writer and the readers of Hebrews had received their knowledge of the gospel not directly from Jesus, but from others who had heard Him (2 : 3) would effectively have ruled out any idea that Peter was the writer, for Peter of all people had received the gospel direct from Jesus Himself; but it has been ingeniously suggested that this could even be true of Peter, for it was Andrew who first accepted Jesus as Master, and who then brought Peter his brother to Him (John 1 : 40, 41). So, it is claimed, it could be said of Peter that he received the gospel in the first place from someone who had received it from Jesus before him. But that suggestion is more ingenious than convincing.

Another suggestion has been made which is related to the suggestion that Peter wrote Hebrews. It has been suggested that, if we cannot attribute Hebrews directly to Peter, we might attribute it to Silvanus (Silas), who was Peter's agent in the writing of his Letter (1 Peter 5 : 12). In this way it is sought to explain the resemblances in the language. But there is no evidence at all that Silas was a man of the intellectual power necessary to write Hebrews, and the resemblance of language can well be explained by the fact that both Peter and the writer to the Hebrews were using ideas and language which were the common property of all Christian writers and thinkers both then and now.

There remain two interesting suggestions at which we must look. One of them is the most imaginative and romantic suggestion, the other is in many ways the most probable, and each is connected with the name of a famous New Testament scholar.

iv. Harnack made the suggestion that Hebrews is the work of Priscilla in conjunction with Aquila. There is no doubt that Priscilla and Aquila were well-known figures in the early Church, and that they were specially near and dear to Paul. He stayed with them in Corinth (Acts 18 : 2, 3). At some time they had even risked their lives for him (Romans 16 : 3, 4). In Ephesus they had a church within their house (1 Corinthians 16 : 19). And they are among those to whom Paul sent his last greetings when the end was near (2 Timothy 4 : 19). It is also possible that Priscilla, or, to give her her more formal name, Prisca, was the more prominent of the two, because in the greeting in Romans her name comes first, and it would be unusual in the ancient world for a wife to be named before her husband. What then are the reasons for suggesting that she and Aquila wrote this Letter? First, the Letter to the Hebrews frequently speaks in the plural, saying "we" and not "I" (e.g. 4 : 11 ; 6 : 9 ; 8 : 1). But it is of course true that this is the way that a preacher often speaks and a writer often writes, especially when there is anything "official" about the statement or the message. Second, it is said that women are specially prominent in the honour roll of Hebrews 11 (11 : 11, 24, 31, 35). Third, it is suggested that this is precisely why Hebrews has no opening address, as all the other New Testament Letters have. Just because Priscilla was a woman she could not begin with greetings in her own name, for women were not supposed to preach or teach at all. Hebrews 11 : 32 is a difficulty for this theory: "Time would fail me to tell . . ."; for there the expression in the Greek is both singular and masculine. But the answer given is that even if for once Priscilla here does slip into the singular and forget Aquila, she still had to write in the masculine, because, being a woman, she was not supposed to be writing at all.

This is the kind of theory which one would like to be true, but in point of fact there is no real evidence for it.

33

v. So we come to the last of the suggestions, the suggestion of Martin Luther, and, as we have said, the most probable suggestion of all. Luther suggested that the author of Hebrews was Apollos. Apollos was a Jew from Alexandria, "an eloquent man, well versed in the Scriptures" (Acts 18 : 24). This is precisely the kind of man who must have written Hebrews. Whoever wrote Hebrews knew the rules of eloquence and rhetoric. He could use assonance and alliteration. "Time would fail me to tell" is a phrase actually used by Demosthenes the great Greek orator (11 : 32). "Now the point in what we are saying is this" is a phrase actually used in Latin by Cicero (8 : 1). This man certainly could write Greek like an orator. Certainly the writer to the Hebrews was "well versed in the Scriptures". He knew his Old Testament as a scholar knows it. And his way of treating Scripture, his way of allegorizing it, of finding types and inner meanings in it, is thoroughly Alexandrian.

But when we have said all this it must still be admitted that to say that Apollos is exactly the kind of man who could have written Hebrews is not in the least to say that he was the man who wrote it, and in fact no one in the early Church ever connected his name with it.

So then these are the main candidates who have been put forward for the authorship of Hebrews. All of the suggestions are interesting; some of them are attractive; but in the last analysis it is best to admit that we do not know who wrote it, that it is the work of some great unknown, and that, as Origen long ago said, the secret of its authorship is known only to God whose Spirit inspired it.

3

IDENTIFYING THE DESTINATION

IF IT IS difficult to identify the writer of the Letter to the Hebrews, it is at least equally difficult to identify its recipients. Even if we were to assume without question that the title *To the Hebrews* is original and correct, it still remains so vague that it would not be a great deal of help. There is only one thing that we can do, and only one source of information in our possession, and that is the Letter itself. So then we must begin by going to the Letter and by trying to see what it has to tell us about the people involved.

The recipients of the Letter are certainly not the Hebrew people at large; they are a perfectly definite community whom the writer of the Letter has visited before and whom he hopes to visit again (13 : 19, 23). They had originally been converted by those who had heard the Lord Himself (2 : 3). That must have been some time ago, for by the time the Letter was written they ought to have reached such an advanced stage of Christianity that they were able to teach others, rather than still be needing elementary teaching themselves (5 : 12). By this time their original leaders were dead, and perhaps they had died for their faith (13 : 7). In the early days they had known trouble. They had had a hard struggle and they had suffered for their faith. They had been exposed to public abuse; some of them at least had been imprisoned; their property had been plundered and they had been ostracized (10 : 32-34); but, however bad things had been, it had not come to the stage of actual martyrdom; they had not yet been called to resist unto blood (12 : 4). And the general indication is that they are very likely to be involved in trouble again.

There is every indication that they were a small and rather select body. They have been, and still are, able to help their fellow Christians; they are generous enough in that, and they cannot have been poor, or such generosity would have been impossible (6 : 10). The very fact that the writer insists that they should have by this time been able to become teachers of others shows that they were not a large, mixed Church of simple and unlettered Christians; they must have been a select group with some kind of special background and some kind of special qualifications which ought to have given them the ability to render special service to the Church (5 : 11-14). It is possible to greet them, as it were, apart from their leaders and apart from the general body of the Church where they were. Through them greetings are sent to the leaders and to the general body of the Christians, of whom they were a part (13 : 24). Apart altogether from these considerations, if the Letter had been written to any of the great Churches in any of the great cities, the address would have been much more definite; the Letter would have been addressed like Paul's Letters to some particular city or town. In a time when the Church necessarily consisted of small groups and house Churches this was perfectly possible. They were a group within a larger group, a special section of the Church, as we might say, a Church within the Church.

Let us now turn to the Letter itself, and let us see what we can learn from it about the spiritual state of the people to whom it was written. We can tell three things about them.

The Correspondents and Their Needs

i. They are people who have received great privileges. How are they to escape judgment and condemnation if they neglect so great a salvation? (2 : 3). They have been enlightened; they have tasted the heavenly gift; they have become partakers of the Holy Spirit; they have tasted the goodness of the word of God and the powers of the age to come (6 : 4, 5). They have received a knowledge of the truth (10 : 26). They are in the position of men to whom God has been very good. God has opened His hand and given them privileges which few have enjoyed. And therein lies their danger, for great privileges bring great responsibilities, and they are in danger of forgetting just that.

ii. This leads us directly to the second fact that the Letter tells us about the people to whom it was written. They are people who are in very serious danger. They are in danger of drifting on to the rocks which will wreck their Christian life (2 : 1). They are in danger of falling away (3 : 12). They are in danger of failing to reach the goal of the promised rest of God, just as the disobedient Israelites in the wilderness lost their opportunity to enter the promised land (4 : 1). If they are not careful, the same sort of disobedience will bring the same penalty (4 : 11). They are in danger of the terrible sin of apostasy, a sin which crucifies Jesus Christ all over again (6 : 6). They are in danger of neglecting to meet together, and of thus neglecting the Christian fellowship of mutual love and encouragement (10 : 25). Their trouble is that there is a certain deliberation about their sin, for they have had so many privileges that they of all people should have known so much better (10 : 26). By their apostasy they are spurning the Son of God and outraging the Spirit of grace (10 : 29). Instead of pressing steadily and courageously forward they are in danger of timorously and faithlessly shrinking back (10 : 39). They are in danger of not even understanding the writer's instruction because they have become sluggish and dull of hearing. By this time they should be so far advanced on the Christian way that they should be teaching others, and instead they are still needing the most elementary instruction (5 : 11-14).

It is the picture of a disillusioned and discouraged group of men, with all the heart and all the adventure gone out of them, a group who are listlessly unwilling to make any effort, a group with heads turned backwards instead of with faces to the wind. They are living in the twilight rather than in the dawn of faith.

iii. The third thing that we can tell about these people is their crying and their clamant need. They need to hold fast their confidence and their pride in their hope to the end (3 : 6, 14). They must hold fast to their Christian confession (4 : 14). They must stop this wavering and get a grip of their faith (10 : 23). They must not be sluggish; they must have the same faith and patience as those who inherited the promises had (6 : 11, 12). The word for *patience* here is *makrothumia*; and *makrothumia*, as one writer put it, was that quality which made the Romans masters of the world, that undefeatability which made them able to lose a battle, but never to lose a campaign or a war, that invincible determination to go on in spite of any setback or any temporary defeat. They must run with patience the race that is set before them (12: 1). Here the word for *patience* is a different word; it is the word *hupomonē*. *Hupomonē* does not describe the patience which can sit down and submissively allow a flood of misfortunes to flow over it; it is not simply the ability to bear things; it is the ability to turn even tragedy into triumph, and gallantly to face anything without losing hope. They must not grow weary or faint-hearted (12 : 3). They must not fall out of the race (12 : 12, 13). They must stick it out to the end.

The need is clear; the need is to hold fast and to hold on in spite of discouragement and trial and pain; the need is to refuse to give up and to give in. The need is to shake themselves out of the listless weariness which has them in its grip. The need is gallantly to face everything in the certainty that it will be worth it in the end.

So then the picture is the picture of men who have received great privileges, of men who have allowed the situation to submerge their hope and their faith, of men whose one need is to take a grip of themselves and a grip of their circumstances and to hold on.

Can we then take this matter one step further and can we identify and localize the people to whom this Letter was first written?

i. We may begin by noting that the Letter never had any other title as far back as we can go than *To the Hebrews*. This is its title in the oldest manuscripts. This is the title in Codex Sinaiticus, Codex Vaticanus, and Codex Alexandrinus; in Codex Ephraem Rescriptus the beginning of Hebrews is missing but this title is given at the end. In the early days no one was sure who the author of the Letter was, but equally no one seemed to doubt that the title of it was correct, and no one ever suggested any other title than *To the Hebrews*. The only alteration that the title underwent was in the later days when it was expanded to include the name of Paul, and it became *The Letter of Paul to the Hebrews*.

But in point of fact this title is of little or no help in determining the destination of the Letter, because the word *Hebrews* had no local significance at all, any more than the word British or American has. It simply meant Hebrew-speaking Jews wherever they might be resident; it is a racial rather than a local name; and since there were Jews scattered all over the world there were Hebrews to be found almost everywhere.

In point of fact Euthalius, one of the early Christian scholars, did take it in this sense, and took the Letter to be addressed to all converted Hebrews, to all Christian Jews, to those of the circumcision all over the world. As we have already seen, this cannot be the case, for it is quite clear from the Letter itself that it was written to some definite, and to indeed some quite small, community. The title of the Letter is not in itself any indication of the place to which the Letter was first sent.

Let us then look at some of the suggestions which have been made to localize these Hebrews. But before we do this we must look at the suggestion that the title is in fact wrong, and that, as it has been put, it does no more than reflect the impression made by the Letter on some early copyist. Moffatt, for instance, believes that the Letter was written to a predominantly Gentile community. He argues that there is no special mention of Jews in it at all, but that it is written to Christians quite generally. He argues that there is no question of a relapse into Judaism, but simply a drift away from Christianity. He argues that the writer's argument is based not on the Temple but on the ancient Tabernacle, and that his knowledge of it is antiquarian and academic and not first hand. He argues that all the quotations are made from the Septuagint, the Greek version of the Old Testament, which at that time was the Bible of every Christian, and not only of the Jews, because of course by that time the New Testament was not yet in existence. He therefore argues that there is nothing specifically Jewish about the Letter at all, and that the title is wrong and misleading.

There is certainly truth in what he says; but it is surely none-theless true that an argument so based on the Tabernacle and on the sacrificial system would have more cogency for Jews than for anyone else.

We may not wish to go quite as far as Westcott, when he brushes aside the suggestion that Hebrews was written to a Gentile audience as no more than an "ingenious paradox", but it does remain true that the concentration of Hebrews upon the sacrificial ritual of Judaism makes it much more appropriate to Jewish readers than to any others. So then let us now turn to consider the places which have been suggested as possible destinations for this Letter.

Alexandria, Rome, Ephesus

ii. It has been suggested that the Letter was originally sent to the Church at Alexandria. In support of that suggestion the following arguments are brought forward.

The Muratorian Canon was the first "official" list of New Testament books, and it listed the books which were regarded as Scripture in the Church at Rome in the latter half of the 2nd Christian century. Now that list does not include the Letter to the Hebrews, but it does have this odd statement: "There is extant also a Letter to the Laodiceans and another to the Alexandrians". No doubt the Letter to the Laodiceans is connected with the Letter to Laodicea mentioned in Colossians 4 : 16. And it is suggested that the Letter to the Alexandrians here referred to, and otherwise lost, may be the Letter to the Hebrews under a different name.

Secondly, it is certainly true that there were a very large number of Jews in Alexandria. Alexandria as a city was divided into five city districts and two out of these five districts were inhabited solely by Jews. A Letter to the Hebrews would certainly have an audience in Alexandria.

Thirdly, the Alexandrian school of Christian scholars were famous for their way of interpreting Scripture allegorically, and for their ability to find inner secret meanings hidden beneath the surface of Scripture. An Alexandrian would treat Scripture exactly as the writer to the Hebrews treats it. To take but one instance, the way in which the writer to the Hebrews finds in the Melchizedek story a forecast and symbol and type of the priesthood of Jesus is thoroughly Alexandrian. The great Jewish Alexandrian scholar was Philo. Philo's aim was to build a bridge between Hebrew and Greek thought; and the way in which he did it was by treating the Old Testament allegorically in order to show that everything that was later to emerge in Greek philosophy was already there, if you could see the inner meanings and read below the surface. It is quite true that the way in which the writer to the Hebrews finds inner meanings in Scripture is characteristically Alexandrian.

Fourthly, if the conjecture that Apollos had something to do with the writing of Hebrews is correct, then Apollos was an Alexandrian, and that might connect the Letter with Alexandria (Acts 18 : 24).

It does seem that a case can be made out for Alexandria. But there is another side to the case.

First, the Church to which the Letter to the Hebrews was written was founded by the apostles or by one of them (2 : 3); no one really knows who founded the Church at Alexandria. The tradition is that Mark was the founder, but certainly none of the apostles has been connected with it.

Second, the group to which the Letter to the Hebrews was written clearly knew Timothy (13 : 23); and it is fairly certain that Timothy never had anything to do with the Church at Alexandria.

Third, as we have already seen, the three great Alexandrian scholars Pantaenus, Clement and Origen all had a great deal to say about Hebrews. They are not at all certain who wrote the Letter, and they certainly do not regard it as a Letter written to their own Church. The Church at Alexandria never connected the Letter to the Hebrews with itself, and if it had been originally a Letter to the Church at Alexandria one would have expected the Alexandrian scholars to be aware of the fact.

It is on the whole not possible to connect Hebrews with Alexandria.

iii. It has been suggested that the Letter was originally sent to a group within the Church at Rome. The following arguments are adduced in favour of that destination.

First, the first person to know and to quote Hebrews, although he does not refer to it by name, is Clement of Rome, writing about the end of the 1st century. So far as our evidence goes, Rome was the first place in which the Letter to the Hebrews was known.

Second, there is one phrase in the Letter which might connect the Letter with Rome. At the very end we have the sentence: "Those who come from Italy send you greetings" (13 : 24). The form of that phrase and of that greeting would make it more likely that the Letter was sent *to* Italy than that it was sent *from* Italy. If I were writing a letter from Glasgow to London, I would not naturally say: "All the people from Glasgow salute you." But if I were writing a letter from London to Glasgow, I might well say: "All the Glasgow people here send you their good wishes." It would then be a greeting from a colony of Glasgow people settled in London to their friends at home. So in the Letter to the Hebrews the sentence: "Those who come from Italy send you greetings", is much more natural if the Letter is being written to Italy from somewhere else, and the writer saying: "The Italians here send you their good wishes." This sentence can be used as an argument that the Letter was written from somewhere abroad to Italy.

There are however very real difficulties in the suggestion that the Letter was written to Rome.

First, although Clement quotes the Letter to the Hebrews, he never quotes it by name, nor does he mention the author. The Roman Church, as we have seen, knew that Paul was not the author of Hebrews, but did not know who was, and for that very reason was for long disinclined to accept the Letter as a part of Scripture. There is no suggestion that the Church at Rome ever regarded Hebrews as their Letter, as they must have done, had it been written to them.

Second, it is not by any means certain that we can say that the Church of Rome was founded by one of the apostles (2 : 3).

Third, and this seems to settle the matter, the writer of Hebrews says to the people to whom he writes: "In your struggle against sin you have not yet resisted to the point of shedding your blood" (12 : 4). If there was one Church of which that could not be said, that Church was the Church at Rome. In the terrible outbreak of violence in A.D. 64, as Westcott puts it, the Roman Church was deluged with the blood of the martyrs. It was in Nero's terrible outburst of savagery that the Christians were rolled in pitch while still alive and used as living torches to light his gardens, that they were sewn up in the skins of animals and flung to the hunting dogs to tear to pieces. Unless Hebrews was written before A.D. 64, this could never have been written of the Roman Church.

There is a case for Rome, but there are difficulties which seem well nigh insurmountable.

iv. One of the most interesting suggestions is the suggestion which connects this Letter with the area around Ephesus in Asia Minor.

There are a number of references in the Letter to the Hebrews which, as it were, stand out from the rest of the Letter. There is the surprisingly large, the at first sight disproportionately large, space allotted to the proof that Jesus is greater than the angels (1 : 5-2 : 16). There is the insistence that Jesus Christ actually and really shared our human nature (2 : 14). There is the insistence that marriage is an honourable estate and that chastity is an essential virtue (13 : 4). The inadequacy of regulations which deal with food and drink and various ablutions, regulations for the body, is pointed out (9 : 10). The recipients of the Letter are "not to be led away by diverse and strange teachings; for it is well that the heart be strengthened by grace, not by foods, which have not benefited their adherents" (13 : 9). There is danger here from some kind of false belief which gives an undue prominence to angels, which belittles the marriage bond, which tends to immorality, which has to do with food and drink, and which can be described as diverse teaching.

Now it so happens that there is another New Testament Letter in which precisely these things occur, and in which precisely these things are a source of error and of danger. That Letter is the Letter to the Colossians. In it the worship of angels is a danger (Colossians 2 : 18). In it strange and complicated teaching masquerading as philosophy is a danger (Colossians 2 : 4, 8). In it regulations about food are a danger (Colossians 2 : 16, 21). In it the real bodily human nature of Jesus Christ is stressed (Colossians 2 : 9).

It could be argued that there is a real similarity between the two Letters. Now the heresy and the mistaken belief behind Colossians is Gnosticism. Gnosticism was a system of thought which began with the basic belief that only spirit is good and that all matter is evil. If all matter is evil, then certain things follow. If matter is evil, then God cannot touch matter. If God cannot touch matter, the only way in which He could create the world and the only way in which He can have any contact with it is through angels, through lesser beings; and so the angels become far too important. If matter is evil, there can be no such thing as a real incarnation. Jesus could not have a material body; He can be no more than a phantom appearance. If matter is evil, then the body is essentially evil. And if the body is evil, you can do one of two things with it. You can either follow a policy of asceticism, beating and starving and neglecting the body, and laying down all kinds of food regulations, or you can say: "The body is evil anyway; nothing will make it good; therefore let it have its own way; sate it and glut; it is evil anyway and it does not matter how you use it." So Gnosticism can issue in deliberate asceticism or in deliberate immorality.

On this view it is Gnosticism which is behind Hebrews; it is the same trouble as is behind Colossians. Both Letters reflect that attitude of mind which sees in the world, not God's creation, but nothing but evil. The Letter to the Hebrews would then be written to show that, so far from being evil, material things, material ritual, material sacrifices, are in fact types and symbols and forecasts which point to the divine realities of God behind them.

If we are to find this kind of thought in Hebrews, we could

44

perhaps assume that it was written to that part of Asia Minor where Colosse was, the area round the great city of Ephesus.

This is an interesting theory, but when we look at it more closely we see that what it has done is that it has taken things which are sidelines and incidental references in Hebrews and has made them the main line of thought in the Letter, and has neglected the whole picture of the Tabernacle ritual which is at the very heart of Hebrews.

The Traditional View

v. We have carefully considered the main claimants to be the recipients of the Letter to the Hebrews; we have looked at Alexandria, at Rome, and at Ephesus; and we have seen that in every instance a case can be put up, and in every instance the case is subject to objections which make it impossible to hold it with any confidence. So, having looked at all the modern conjectures, we must look again at the view of tradition, for it may well be that there is at least as much to be said for the traditional view of Hebrews as there is for any other of the views.

The traditional view, which we find, for instance, in the ancient commentators like Chrysostom and Theodoret, is that Hebrews was written to the Palestinian Jews, and especially to the Jews of Jerusalem. These early commentators produce one very odd argument. In 3 : 1 the writer addresses his readers as "holy brethren" (*adelphoi hagioi*), brethren who, to give the word its A.V. translation, are saints. And the older commentators make the curious statement that the Jerusalem Church is the only Church which can be addressed as "holy brethren", for it was specially the Church of the saints, since it was the Church founded by Jesus Himself. We may disregard that as a curiosity of criticism. But what is to be said for Jerusalem as the destination of this Letter? What is to be said for the view that it was originally sent to Jewish Palestinian Christians?

(a) There is the fact that this is the tradition and that the Letter, as we have seen, never bore any other title than *To the*

Hebrews. Now this title would suit the Church at Jerusalem better than any other Church. Eusebius quotes authority that up to the time of Hadrian the Jerusalem Church was "solely composed of Hebrews", and that all its bishops were "of the circumcision" (*The Ecclesiastical History* 4 . 5; 6 . 14). The Clementine Homilies speak of "the Church of the Hebrews in Jerusalem" (*Clementine Homilies* 11 : 35). We cannot, of course, argue that the title *To the Hebrews* is original, but what we can state as a fact is that the Letter throughout all the time that it has been known has never had any other title, and that that title best suits the Church at Jerusalem.

(b) The subject matter best suits Jewish readers. Not only does it best suit Jewish readers at large, but it also best suits Jews who were absolutely devoted to the Temple and to its priestly and sacrificial ritual. The Jews to whom this Letter is addressed are not primarily interested in the Law; their interest is in the Temple.

It is perfectly true that the ritual which is discussed and interpreted is the ritual of the Tabernacle. But there are three things to be said about this. First, the Jew characteristically and instinctively carried his institutions as far back as possible. And it is the Tabernacle ritual which is the Mosaic ritual, and it would be that Mosaic ritual which he would take as the real sacrificial ritual of Israel. Second, it was the Tabernacle which was the real type and model of sacrificial ritual; true, the Temple was the great representative of that model; but the ultimate pattern goes back to the Tabernacle. Third, in the dreams of the restoration of the glory of Israel it was the Tabernacle which was to be restored (2 Maccabees 2 : 4ff.). The fact that the ritual which is discussed and depicted and interpreted is the Tabernacle ritual is perfectly natural for a devout Jew.

It would then seem that this Letter's subject matter suits best of all people whose lives and hearts are intertwined with the Temple worship. The exiled Jews of Egypt did build a Temple at Leontopolis and did re-enact the sacrificial ritual there, and therefore some people have connected this Letter with Egypt and Alexandria, as we have already seen. But the Temple at

Leontopolis never took the place of the Temple at Jerusalem even for the Alexandrian Jews. A Letter whose subject matter is so saturated with the sacrificial and priestly ritual is more relevant to Jerusalem than to anywhere else.

(c) What then is the situation? Let us try to reconstruct the spiritual life of a Jew who was converted to Christianity in the earliest days. In the very earliest days Church and Temple, so to speak, coexisted. We find Peter and John on the way to the Temple at the hour of prayer, as the most natural thing in the world, and we find them preaching in the Temple courts as the obvious place in which to preach (Acts 3 : 1). At first there was no reason why a man should stop going to the Temple because he had begun to go to the Church. So there was an age of transition in Jerusalem. But bit by bit something began to emerge. As Westcott puts it, it began to be clear that devotion to the Temple ritual was not an innocent extra; it was something which obscured the real meaning of Christianity. A religion of grace cannot be a religion of animal sacrifice; a religion based on the triumphant adequacy of Jesus Christ cannot have additions to Him and to His sacrifice. And so there came the time when there had to be a clean break. To quote Westcott again, to be in exactly the same position at the end of an age of transition as you were at the beginning of it may be nothing less than apostasy from the truth. It may well be sin not to make the onward move which should be made.

The Hebrews' Loss and Gain

Here then is our situation. The lives of these Jews had been centred on the Temple; the sacrificial system had been to them the most precious thing in life; for a time Temple and Church coexisted; but then came the inexorable necessity for the break. They made it; they did not need to make it from choice; the Temple would banish them from its precincts anyway. The better men understood Christianity, the bigger the rift between Church and Temple—and the Temple saw that just as clearly as

47

the Church. The break had been made—and there were those who were far more impressed with what they had lost than with what they had gained. The splendour of the Temple, the magnificence of its liturgy and ritual, the spiritual comfort of the sacrifices, the essence of Judaism, all that they and their fathers had loved and had indeed died for—it was gone. And there were those who like their forefathers in the wilderness longed to go back.

Here is the situation. The writer to the Hebrews is showing to men who had lost much that they had gained more. He is showing them that, even if they had lost the Temple and its sacrifices, they had gained the great High Priest and His all-sufficient sacrifice made once and for all.

This makes sense. What is the objection to it? There are objections.

(a) The writer of the Letter to the Hebrews thinks in Greek. When he quotes, he quotes the Septuagint, the Greek Old Testament, even when it differs from the Hebrew. Would such a Hellenist approach really appeal to Palestinian Jews of Jerusalem? Would this Hellenism appeal to those who thought in Hebrew?

(b) It is not possible to say of the Jerusalem Church that it was founded by the apostles and not by Jesus Himself (2 : 3).

(c) It is not possible to say of the Jerusalem Church that it had not resisted unto blood (12 : 4). It had certainly known persecution and it had certainly seen Stephen die a martyr's death.

(d) It is clear that the people to whom this Letter is written were able and willing to help others (6 : 10); they were not poverty stricken; and the Jerusalem Church was so poor that one of Paul's dearest undertakings was to organize the collection for it from other Churches (Romans 15 : 25, 26).

(e) It is hardly likely that it was necessary to urge the Jerusalem Church not to forget its great leaders, such as James the brother of our Lord (13 : 7).

Here we have a very puzzling situation. On the one hand there is so much that suits Jerusalem as it suits no other place; on the other hand there are certain difficulties which cannot be waved away. Is there no way of resolving this dilemma?

Spicq, the French commentator, has made a suggestion which seems to us to have the solution in it.

The New Testament writers are always supremely careful to make their writing relevant for their readers. They choose their pictures, their metaphors, their illustrations from a world which is their readers' world. Jesus began this with His parables and all subsequent New Testament teaching maintained this accent on relevance. Now, if that be so, *for whom is the Letter to the Hebrews most relevant?* It is a Letter which is based on the priesthood and the sacrificial system. For whom is such a Letter most relevant?

The Priestly Body

The answer is obvious. *Such a Letter is supremely relevant to a body of priests.* And now the key question—*Is there any indication in the story of the early Church that there was such a body of priests?*

There most certainly is. Just after the story of the setting apart of the Seven, there comes the verse (Acts 6 : 7):

> And the word of God increased; and the number of the disciples multiplied greatly in Jerusalem, and a great many of the priests were obedient to the faith.

Here we have the group to whom of all people the Letter to the Hebrews would be most intensely relevant. The Temple and its ritual and liturgy was their life. At the highest their devotional life was realized in it; at the lowest they had a prestige and they had perquisites and they had a life which no man would willingly give up. It may be that at first they tried to be priests and Christians; it may be that at first they tried to serve both Church and Temple; and then there came the heart-breaking rift. They had to choose, and some were regretting their choice, some were feeling that they had lost too much.

This will explain so much. While the Jerusalem Church as a whole was poor, they at first had their vast perquisites out of which they could help. At first they had not been involved in trouble; that for them was to come later. With their tradition and their culture and their education and their knowledge of the sacred book, were they not abundantly qualified to become teachers of the Church? When they came to look back and to realize what they had lost were they not likeliest of all to be haunted by the desire to go back? Further, if the Letter to the Hebrews was written just before the fall of Jerusalem and the destruction of the Temple, it was just then that Jewish nationalism was most intense; it was probably just then that into the Synagogue prayers were inserted the cursing of the *minim*, the Gentiles, the Christians. How must a priest have felt when he knew he was being cursed by his fellow Jews in the daily prayer of their worship? Surely here is the very situation we need.

We may even fit in the likelihood that this Letter was written to Rome, and even the Hellenistic character of it. It may be that some quite small group of these priests emigrated to Rome, for there were thousands of Jews in Rome, and the time would come when they would have to emigrate for the sake of their very lives. It may be that there in Rome they lived as a little group and that a great despairing depression had settled on them. And it may be that just then some great soul found them and wrote to them out of his love and pastoral care for them to lift up their hearts.

No one can prove this for certain. But it may well be that the Letter to the Priesthood was written to a little group of priests, exiled in a foreign land, and for the moment weighed down with the sense of all that they had lost; and in it the unknown writer sets before them the glory and the wonder that they had gained.

4

IDENTIFYING THE FORM AND THE DATE

WHOEVER THE WRITER to the Hebrews was, he wrote with a care and with a skill which give his book a technical excellence from the point of view of Greek which is unexcelled in the New Testament.

There have been those who have found in Hebrews—and very possibly rightly—the technical form which a Greek orator would have used for a carefully composed speech. Fully fashioned Greek oratorical speeches fell into four divisions, each with its own name and aim, and it is possible to distinguish these four sections in the work of the writer to the Hebrews.

1. There was the *Prooimion*, which leads up to the main thesis and in which the main thesis is simply expressed. In Hebrews the *prooimion* is in 1 : 1—4 : 13, and then in 4 : 14-16 the whole theme of the work is shortly and simply set out.

2. There was the *Diēgēsis*, in which there is a preliminary treatment of the main doctrinal theme followed by a preliminary exhortation. In Hebrews the *diēgēsis* runs from 5 : 1—6 : 20.

3. There is the *Apodeixis*, in which there is a fuller and more developed treatment of the doctrinal theme. In Hebrews the *apodeixis* stretches from 7 : 1—10 : 18.

4. Finally, there is the *Epilogos*, in which there is a fuller exhortation to accept and to live the demands which the doctrinal part brings. In Hebrews the *epilogos* runs from 10 : 19—13 : 21.

It can hardly be accidental that these four divisions are so easily identifiable in the work of this writer. He was a skilled writer and teacher and speaker, and he uses with skill and ability the forms which he knew and in which he was trained.

But as in so many other things Hebrews presents us with a problem as to what its form in fact is. The problem is plain for all to see. The problem is that Hebrews has an epistolary ending but it has no epistolary beginning. It ends like a letter, but it does not begin like one. It ends with a section obviously addressed to a particular group of people, but it does not, like all the Pauline Letters, begin by identifying the people to whom it is written. There are two possible explanations of this.

i. It could be a letter which for some reason or other has lost its beginning, or the beginning of which for some reason or other was never written or was perhaps even suppressed. We have already seen that this is the view that Harnack took. He suggested that the main author of the work was Priscilla in conjunction with her husband Aquila, and that because she was a woman and because it was considered improper that a woman should write instruction like this, the beginning of the Letter was completely omitted.

The trouble about that suggestion is that Hebrews does not read as if it had ever begun any other way than the way in which it does begin. To prefix anything to its magnificent and sonorous beginning would simply have been to spoil it. It could not begin more impressively than it does begin. Beyond doubt Hebrews begins as its writer meant it to begin.

ii. We are then left with the second alternative, which is that Hebrews did not begin as a letter at all, but that it began as a speech, an address, a homily, which would have been personally and verbally spoken by the writer of it to his friends, if it had been possible for him to do so; but, being separated from them, he sent the homily in writing, and added a kind of covering letter at the end of it.

Homily or Sermon?

If this is the case then the homily proper covers the first twelve chapters. 13 : 1-9 is practical advice; 13 : 10-16 is a final restatement of the main theme; 13 : 17-19 resumes the practical advice; 13 : 20, 21 is the blessing; and 13 : 22-25 is a very brief covering note.

Here is the explanation which covers the facts. For some reason the writer to the Hebrews was separated from his friends, and was unable at the time to come to them. He knew their condition; he knew what he would have said had he been able to speak to them face to face; and so in his absence he wrote out his sermon and sent it to them, so that at least to some extent the written might take the place of the spoken word. Hebrews is the homily or sermon of a pastor who had to send in writing what circumstances prevented him from saying face to face.

Identifying the Date

A modern letter or a modern book usually bears its date printed or written on it, but it is very seldom that any ancient literary document has any mention of its own date. The date has to be worked out by references to the book in other writings and by such hints and indications as its own contents will provide.

A Fixed Point

In regard to the Letter to the Hebrews we can start with one fixed point. It is quoted by Clement of Rome in his First Letter to the Corinthians, and that Letter was most probably written somewhere about A.D. 95. The Letter to the Hebrews therefore must have been written before A.D. 95, and probably quite some time before that, because it normally takes a book a little time to acquire that literary status which causes it to be quoted in other books. As an outside limit then we may say that the Letter to the Hebrews was written some time before A.D. 95. It cannot be later than that, but how much earlier is it? Are there any indications in the Letter itself which will enable us to date it?

i. It has been pointed out that the Letter has no mention of elders, deacons or bishops. The only such people who are mentioned are the *leaders* (*proēgoumenoi*) (13 : 7, 17), and *pro-ēgoumenoi* is an ordinary, simple, non-official, non-ecclesiastical word, meaning simply, as it is translated, *leaders*. Now there have been those who have argued that, because Hebrews has no mention of Church officials of any kind, it must therefore be very early and that it must come from a time when the Church had no organization at all. But in point of fact there was practically never a time like that, for according to the story of Acts Paul appointed elders in his Churches as soon as there were Christian groups of any kind at all (Acts 14 : 23).

What is much more likely is that the group to which Hebrews was written, the group of ex-priests, did not have any ecclesiastical organization, because they were not a congregation but only a group within a congregation and in a letter to such a group you would not expect to find references to Church officials; you would expect to find simply their leaders addressed.

ii. There are in the Letter certain references to persecution which ought to help us to fix the date.

In the earliest days of their faith the people to whom the Letter was written had had to undergo struggles, sufferings, abuse. Some of them apparently had been in prison, and some of them had had their homes and property attacked and plundered (10 : 32-34). It sounds as if some of their early leaders had died for their faith (13 : 7). And yet as a whole it was still true that they had not yet been called to resist unto blood; red martyrdom had never been demanded from them as a Church (12 : 4). This is to say that the Letter comes from a time when Christians had had to suffer abuse and unpopularity and personal attack, but when as yet they had not as a whole been faced with the threat of dying for their faith, although it may be that certain of their leaders had been faithful unto death.

In the Jerusalem Church persecution came very early, for it came immediately after the death of Stephen about A.D. 34. At that stage in that persecution in which Paul was prominent it is not said that the Christians died for their faith, but it does say that Paul laid waste the Church, invaded the houses of the Christians and dragged them off to prison. Now this fits both our facts and our deductions about Hebrews. This is exactly the kind of persecution which Hebrews 10 : 32-34 speaks about, and it is exactly at the right time, for it was just then that the priests had come into the Church (Acts 6 : 7). It may well be that here we have the persecution of the first days which the writer to the Hebrews calls to memory.

The Persecution of Nero

Now we saw further the only place with which the Letter is in so many words connected is Italy (13 : 24). And we saw that it is possible that a group of these converted priests had found their way to Rome. Now this much is quite certain, that, if it was possible to say to any group within the Roman Church that they had not yet resisted unto blood, the time must have been before A.D. 64 when the fury of the persecution of Nero fell on the Christian Church.

We have here just such a situation as fits the facts, and we may reconstruct it as follows. The priests had been converted in the days of Stephen, and at that time the fury of the young Paul had involved them in abuse, in the plundering of their homes and in imprisonment. They had left Jerusalem; they had "gone forth outside the camp bearing abuse for him" (13 : 13); and they had settled amidst their fellow Jews in Rome. As we have seen, for a while they did not realize how radical this break was. The years passed; the first enthusiasm faded and cooled; the magnificence and the splendour of what they had lost began to haunt them; the bleakness of the earthly future began to daunt them; and now almost thirty years after their hearts had first been moved they are wondering if they have done right and their hearts are turning back. In this way we would get a date sometime in the very early sixties of the 1st century for our Letter.

iii. There is something further which may well support this. It seems quite certain that the Letter to the Hebrews must have been written prior to A.D. 70 when the Temple at Jerusalem was destroyed in the war with Rome. If the Temple had been destroyed, it is surely quite certain that the writer to the Hebrews would have spoken of the fact. It would have surely seemed to him that this was indeed the judgment of God on all the ancient ritual; it would have seemed to him that this was the action of God making it impossible to go back.

Further, the writer to the Hebrews consistently speaks of the Temple worship as still going on. "Here tithes are received by mortal men" (7 : 8). "They serve a copy and shadow of the heavenly sanctuary" (8 : 5). In 9 : 6-9 the whole ritual of the sacrificial system and of the Day of Atonement is spoken of as if it was still going on. In 13 : 10 the distinction is drawn between the altar of the Christian and the altar of the Jewish priesthood.

The Most Likely Date

There are two points of objection to be met. First, it is perfectly true that it is the worship of the Tabernacle about which the writer to the Hebrews speaks; but, as we have already seen, he does so because it is the Mosaic system of priesthood and sacrifice in which he is interested, and that Mosaic system, even if it was originally attached to the Tabernacle, was now exemplified in the worship of the Temple. To the writer to the Hebrews the worship of the Temple was the worship of the Tabernacle in his own time. Second, the New Testament has a way of speaking of things which are demonstrably past as still existing in the present. For instance, the Fourth Gospel has it: "Now there is in Jerusalem by the sheep gate a pool, in Hebrew called Bethzatha" (John 5 : 2). The Fourth Gospel was written about A.D. 100; Jerusalem had been destroyed in A.D. 70 and the gate and the pool had ceased to exist except as ruins; and yet for the purposes of his story the writer of the Fourth Gospel uses the present tense.

But this is not parallel to the usage of the writer to the Hebrews. He is speaking of a way to God which is still used by people although it is quite inadequate and although a better way has been provided in Jesus Christ. He is speaking of a situation in which men are actually using another way to try to approach God, a way which can never be effective. It seems to us essential for the argument of the writer to the Hebrews that the levitical priesthood and the levitical sacrifices are still a rival system to Jesus Christ, the true High Priest and the true and only sacrifice, and, if this is so, the Letter to the Hebrews must of necessity be dated before A.D. 70.

All the facts converge to show that the most likely date for the Letter to the Hebrews is in the very early sixties of the 1st century, before the Neronic persecution and before the destruction of the Temple. Hebrews will therefore belong to the same time as the Letters of Paul.

5

CHILD OF TWO WORLDS

THE WRITER TO the Hebrews was a child of two worlds, and, although these two worlds would have put it differently, basically and fundamentally they were both searching for the same thing. As Philo once put it: "All religion comes to its perfection in the vision of God" (*Quis rer. div. her. sit* 1 . 508). The search of the soul, no matter how it is expressed, is ultimately the search for God.

Now it so happened that the writer to the Hebrews wrote out of a background of thought in which this search for God was impossibly difficult, or he wrote out of a background in which men were haunted by the thought of the utter transcendence of God. They could think only of the vast, unbridgeable gulf between God and man. The very adjective by which God is most commonly described, the adjective *holy*, basically means *different*, *other*. God in Otto's phrase is *The Wholly Other*. How then can man have any contact, much less any communion, with the God who is utterly transcendent and the essentially other? Maximus of Tyre wrote of God: "He who is older than the sun, older than the sky, greater than time and lapse of time and the whole stream of nature is unnamed by legislators, and unspoken by the voice unseen by the eyes" (*Diss.* 8 . 9). Plato, he says, cannot tell us of this God. "His name he does not tell us, for he knew it not; nor does he tell us his colour, for he saw him not; nor his size, for he touched him not . . . the Deity himself is unseen by sight, unspoken by the voice, untouched by fleshly touch, unheard by the hearing" (*Diss.* 17 . 9). "He is by himself," said Plotinus, "abiding still and beyond all things" (*Enneades* 5 . 1 . 6). Philo writes of the searcher: "Wisdom leads him first into the antechamber of the Divine Reason, and when he is there he does not at once enter into the Divine Presence; but sees him afar off, or rather not even afar off can he behold him, but only he sees that place where he stands is still infinitely far from the unnamed, unspeakable, and uncomprehensible God" (*De Somn.* 1 . 11).

Jewish and Greek

The writer to the Hebrews wrote out of both a Jewish and a Greek background, and in both these backgrounds we find this conviction of the transcendence of God.

In the Old Testament we find the idea that it is dangerous, even fatal, to approach God, that to approach God is to die. Moses hears the voice of God say: "You cannot see my face; for man shall not see me and live" (Exodus 33 : 20). After the giving by God and receiving by Moses of the ten commandments it is the astonished exclamation of the people: "We have this day seen God speak with man and man still live" (Deuteronomy 5 : 24). After the Peniel experience Jacob says in amazement: "I have seen God face to face, and yet my life is preserved" (Genesis 32 : 30). It is Manoah's terrified cry to his wife after he has discovered who his visitor was: "We shall surely die, for we have seen God" (Judges 13 : 22). It is God's word to Gideon when Gideon is terrified that he has seen the angel of the Lord: "Peace be to you; do not fear, you shall not die" (Judges 6 : 23). Even the High Priest is not to enter the Holy of Holies at all times, but only on the Day of Atonement, "lest he die" (Leviticus 16 : 2).

It is exactly here that the function of the priest in Jewish religion emerges. Sacrifice could be offered in the Temple and nowhere else. A Jew would provide his own sacrifice, but he would not make his own sacrifice; that was the function of the priest. In the Temple there was a series of Courts, the Court of the Gentiles, beyond which a Gentile could not go; the Court of the Women, beyond which a woman could not go; the Court of the Israelites, beyond which an ordinary Israelite could not go; then finally the Court of the Priests in which the altar of the burnt-offering stood, and at the back of which there rose the

Temple proper, the Holy Place and the Holy of Holies; into the Court of the Priests only a priest could go, and into the Holy of Holies only the High Priest could go, and that only once a year. This whole lay-out makes it quite clear that the priest is the representative of the people in regard to entry into the presence of God. In the priest the people enter the presence of God, and in the person of the High Priest the whole nation enters the presence of God. The Latin for priest is *pontifex*, which means *bridge-builder*; it was the priest who was held to build the bridge across the gulf between man and God.

So in Judaism there was the sense of the transcendence of God, the conviction that it was dangerous and even fatal to approach God, and the belief that the priest, and especially the High Priest, was the representative of the people in the presence of God.

We now turn to the Greek world. Ever since Plato the Greeks had drawn a line of distinction between the real and the unreal world; and the important thing about this distinction was that, as Plato had seen it, the world in which we live, the world which we see and touch and taste and handle, is the unreal world; the real world is unseen and beyond. Further, it was Plato's belief that in the unseen world beyond there rest the perfect ideas, the perfect forms, the perfect patterns, of which this visible world is the shadowy and the imperfect copy. According to Plato, everything has its perfect form or idea in the unseen world. So, to take a very simple example, in the unseen world there is the form, the idea, of a chair, of which all visible and material chairs are imperfect copies.

This means that the seen and the visible and the earthly are the unreal, and the unseen and the invisible are the real. This means that in this world we have nothing but shadows and copies; it is in the unseen world that the real forms and ideas dwell. As Plato put it: "The creator of the world had designed and carried out his work according to an unchangeable and eternal pattern of which the world is but a copy" (*Timaeus* 28C, 29B). As Philo puts it: "God knew from the beginning that a fair copy could never come into being apart from a fair pattern, and that none of the objects perceivable by sense could be flawless which was not modelled after an archetype and the spiritual idea, and thus, when he prepared to create this visible world, he shaped beforehand the world of ideas in order to constitute the corporeal after the incorporeal and the godlike pattern" (*De Op. Mundi* 16). Ideas, Seneca wrote to Lucilius, were "what all visible things were created from, and what formed the pattern for all things" (*Letters* 57 . 18 . 19). The idea is the eternal and everlasting pattern of the changing things of time. This is as true of conceptions as it is of things. Cicero said: "We have no real and life-like likeness of real law and genuine justice; all that we enjoy is a shadow and a sketch" (*De Offic.* 3 . 17).

The problem, therefore, for the Greek was how to get to reality, how to get beyond the shadows and the copies to the real things, how to get from the imperfect earthly copies to the divine ideas. Now the Greek would have taken it as a first principle that no man ever can reach reality so long as he is in the body. *Sōma sēma*, the body is a tomb, ran the Orphic jingle. The body is a house of detention in which the soul is imprisoned, said Philolaus (*Fr.* 13). The study of philosophy is nothing other than the study of dying (Plato, *Phaedo* 64-67). Epictetus described himself as "a poor soul shackled to a corpse" (*Fr.* 23). Seneca speaks of "the detestable habitation" of the body, of the vain flesh in which the soul is imprisoned while it pines for its celestial home (*Letters* 92 . 110). The sage who wrote Wisdom felt exactly the same: "The corruptible body presses down upon the soul and the earthly tabernacle weighs down the mind that muses upon many things" (Wisdom 9 : 15).

Here then is the Greek problem. The problem is to get from the unreal to the real. The real is in the world beyond, and no man will ever reach reality so long as he is weighed down by the earthly body; he must wait until he has sloughed it off. On the pedestal of Newman's statue in London there is the inscription *ab umbris et imaginibus ad veritatem*, from the shadows and the semblances to the truth, the implication being that only after death does a man enter into reality—and that is exactly what the Greeks would have said.

Here then is the problem. It is basically the same problem although it is expressed in a different way. The Hebrew would ask: How can I approach God? How can I bridge that unbridgeable gap? And, even if I could bridge it, how can I in my sinful inadequacy stand in the presence of the holiness of God? The Greek would ask: How can I reach reality? How can I pass beyond the shadows of earth to the realities of heaven? How can I get behind the earthly copies that I can see to the eternal ideas that I cannot see? And the claim of the writer to the Hebrews is quite clear; his claim is that through Jesus Christ, and through Jesus Christ alone, we have access to God and access to reality. In Him we reach the true tabernacle which God pitched and not men (8 : 2); in Him we reach the things that cannot be shaken (12 : 27); in Him we reach the city whose maker and builder is God (11 : 10). We have a better hope by which we can draw near to God (7 : 19). The very text on which he writes his whole letter is, "Let us draw near" (10 : 22). Jesus Christ alone is the way to reality and to God. Be a man Jew, or be a man Greek, in Jesus Christ his search is ended. Whether life is to be regarded as the philosophic search for reality or the religious search for God, the search finds its goal in Jesus Christ.

6

THE SUPREMACY OF JESUS CHRIST

WE HAVE SEEN the height of the claim that the writer to the Hebrews makes for Jesus Christ. In Him, he claims, the search of the heart and the quest of the mind find their goal. It is with this assertion that he begins his letter, and the opening chapters are his proof of it.

i. He begins (1 : 1-4) by proving that Jesus is superior to the prophets. The revelation which came by the prophets was *in many and various ways* (1 : 1). It was, as the Greek has it, *polumerōs* and *polutropōs*; *polumerōs* literally means *in many parts*, and *polutropōs* literally means *in many ways* or *in many methods*. The revelation which came by the prophets was necessarily partial and fragmentary, for no prophet had the whole of the truth, but each had his own part and share in it. The revelation which came by the prophets had necessarily to fit itself to the age and time and generation of each of the prophets. They had to use the temporary symbols and pictures and conceptions in which eternal truth could be expressed for their own temporary conditions. In the nature of things the revelation which came by the prophets was fragmentary in its content and temporary in its expression.

But with Jesus Christ it is very different. He is in a special relationship to the universe, to men, and to God.

(a) He is the *creator* of the universe, for by Him all things were made (1 : 2). He is the *sustainer* of the universe, for by Him all things are upheld (1 : 3). He is the *goal* of the universe, for God has made Him the heir of all things (1 : 2). In Jesus Christ the universe had its beginning; on Him it depends for its continuance; in Him it will find its consummation. All things began, continue and will end in Him.

(b) He is the *purifier* of men. He made purification for the sins of men (1 : 3). He made *katharismon*; that is to say, he makes a man *katharos*, which means *pure*, in the particular sense of being made fit to enter into the presence of God. It is only in Jesus Christ that the way to God is opened for sinful men.

(c) He is *Son* of God. In these last days God spoke not by a human agent, however inspired, but by one who was a Son, by one whose union with Himself was far beyond anything into which any man could enter. That union is expressed in two ways. He *reflects* the glory of God; He is the *apaugasma* of the glory of God (1 : 3). In Him we see God as in a mirror; in Him we see the glory that streams from the radiance of God. He is the *very stamp*, the *charaktēr*, of God's nature (1 : 3). *Charaktēr* is the Greek word for the impression that a seal makes in wax. The impression corresponds exactly to the seal; the impression tells you exactly what the seal is like. Even so in Jesus Christ we see exactly what God is like. Furthermore He shares the very throne of God (1 : 4).

The Splendour of Christ

So the writer to the Hebrews sets before us the splendour of Jesus Christ, a splendour compared with which the revelation of even the greatest of the prophets is partial, fragmentary, incomplete, and necessarily limited to its time.

ii. The writer to the Hebrews then goes on to prove the superiority of Jesus Christ over the angels. To us it might well seem that to do this is quite unnecessary, and that this superiority is not in question; but for the writer to the Hebrews and his readers this was a living issue. He was writing at a time when men were haunted by the transcendence of God. Their minds were weighted down with the sense of the difference, the distance, the otherness of God. In such a mental climate it was only natural that men should seek for intermediaries between them and God. If God could neither be known nor met directly and personally, then it was necessary to find some connecting link between Him and men. So at this time the Jews had a highly developed angelology. Every nation had its angel; every man and every child had his angel; every natural force, the winds and the rain and the fire, had its angel. So all-pervading had this doctrine of angels become that it could be said that "every blade of grass has its angel".

The Greek world had always tended to hold, as Plutarch held, that "they do God no honour who involve Him in the affairs of men and of the world". The Greeks increasingly thought of God as distant and detached in order to preserve His perfect serenity and peace. They therefore introduced between man and God a kind of protective layer of *daimons*, who were not demons in the English sense of the term, but who were intermediate beings between God and men. The Gnostic tendency of thought completely separated matter and spirit, holding that matter is essentially evil, and spirit essentially good. This meant that God, who is pure spirit, can have no contact whatever with matter, and so once again we arrive at a world view in which a series of intermediaries between God and man is a necessity. In such a world it was no waste of time to set beyond all doubt the superiority of Jesus Christ to these all-pervading intermediate powers. So to this proof the writer to the Hebrews sets himself, and, as he does so, he confirms every step of it with an appropriate quotation from the Old Testament.

(a) It is true that sometimes the angels are collectively called the sons of God (Job 1 : 6); but no angel is ever called the Son of God; and yet this is precisely what Jesus is called (Hebrews 1 : 5 ; Psalm 2 : 7 ; 2 Samuel 7 : 14). The sonship of Jesus Christ is something unique, unshared by any other being.

(b) No angel is ever worshipped (Hebrews 1 : 6); in fact they are to worship the Son (Deuteronomy 32 : 43, in the Septuagint version ; Psalm 97 : 7). Reverence is the prerogative of the Son.

(c) The angels are servants, themselves created, and therefore changeable and perishable; the Son is divine, exalted, the creator, who will remain when all things have passed away (Hebrews 1 : 8-12 ; Psalm 104 : 4 ; 45 : 6, 7 ; 102 : 25-27). The angels are part of creation which is necessarily evanescent; the Son is of that order of being which is uncreated, and which is above the changes and the chances of life and time.

65

(d) The ultimate victory, triumph and supremacy belongs to the Son (Hebrews 1 : 13 ; Psalm 110 : 1). In the end all things will be subjected to Him, and He will reign supreme. The angels are really no more than servants who exist only to help those to whom the salvation of God is sent.

(e) It is not to angels that all things are subjected (Hebrews 2 : 5-9 ; Psalm 8 : 4-6), it is to the Son. True, He had to pass through humiliation and death, but it is that very suffering which has given Him the place which is the highest of all.

So then the superiority of the Son to the angels is set beyond a doubt.

iii. Next the writer to the Hebrews moves on to prove the superiority of the Son over Moses (3 : 1-6). Again, we might think that this is unnecessary, but we must remember the place that Moses held in Jewish thought. The Law was the most precious possession of Israel; the Law was divine, the very voice of God, and it was through Moses that this Law came. Nothing better illustrates the place of Moses in Jewish thought than his appearance in the Transfiguration story (Matthew 17 : 3; Mark 9 : 4 ; Luke 9 : 30). Moses appears with Elijah, because they are the two supreme representative figures of Jewish religion; they stand for the Law and the prophets. Ben Sirach said of Moses: "God made him equal in glory to the holy ones" (Ecclesiasticus 45 : 2).

So the writer to the Hebrews does not deny for a moment the greatness of Moses. But Moses was faithful as a *servant*; Jesus Christ is faithful as the *Son* (3 : 5). Great as is the glory of a great house, the glory of the builder and the architect of it is greater yet; and the glory of Moses is the glory of the house, the glory of the Son is the glory of the builder of it (3 : 3, 4).

Jewish religion reached its peak in Moses, but that peak is overpassed in the still greater revelation in Jesus Christ.

The New Priesthood

iv. Finally, in the matter of superiority, the writer to the Hebrews comes to the claim which to him was the most important claim of all. Jesus is superior to the Aaronic priesthood. Here indeed is something. It was in and through the priesthood that the people approached God; but the approach which Jesus Christ offered was far greater and far more effective. We shall very soon be dealing with the idea in much more detail; at the moment we note certain basic ideas in it.

There are certain basic essentials for a priest. He must be so one with the people whom he represents that he can sympathize with them in their weakness and in their need (5 : 2). It is just such a priest that we have in Jesus Christ, one who can sympathize with our weakness, for He was tempted in all things even as we are tempted, though He was without sin (4 : 15). He is like His brothers in all things, and because He Himself suffered He is able to help others who are going through it (4 : 10-18). It is in fact in that very suffering and that deep involvement in the human situation that the greatness of Jesus Christ lies (4 : 10 ; 5 : 7-10). The priest must be one with his people and Jesus Christ supremely is that.

No priest takes the high office of the priesthood to himself; to it he must be called by God as Aaron was (5 : 4). Even so, Jesus did not exalt Himself, but His appointment to His perfect priesthood was by God (5 : 5, 6).

But in the case of the earthly and the levitical priesthood the inadequacy of the priest is immediately seen in the simple fact that the priest has to offer sacrifice for his own sin before ever he can offer sacrifice for the sin of the people (5 : 3 ; 7 : 27). The earthly priest is a sinning man amongst sinning men, but Jesus Christ had no need to offer any sacrifice for Himself, for He had no sin.

The business of the priest is to offer sacrifice (5 : 1 ; 8 : 3); that is why he exists. But just as the priest is an imperfect man, so all that he can offer is an imperfect sacrifice. It is an animal sacrifice (9 : 13 ; 10 : 3, 4). In the first place, no such sacrifice can ever really cleanse a man's heart and conscience (9 : 9, 10). In the second place, the essentially unavailing character of earthly sacrifice is made abundantly clear by the fact that earthly sacrifices have to be made over and over again (9 : 25 ; 10 : 1,

2, 11). The levitical sacrifices are clearly not doing what they are intended to do, for day in and day out they have to be made and remade.

So in the case of the earthly levitical sacrifices the priest is imperfect because he has first to offer sacrifice for his own sin, and the sacrifice is imperfect, for no animal sacrifice can ever cleanse the conscience and every earthly sacrifice has to be made over and over again throughout the years. How different is Jesus Christ! He is the perfect priest who needs to make no offering for His own sin. And, further, and even greater, He brings the perfect sacrifice. That perfect sacrifice is Himself (9 : 12), and what He offers is not the flesh and blood of animals, it is that perfect obedience which is the only true sacrifice and the only sacrifice God desires and accepts (10 : 5-10). The result of all this is the perfect offering made by the perfect priest; the offering of Himself by Jesus Christ is made once and for all and never needs to be made again (9 : 12, 26, 28 ; 10 : 10, 12, 14).

Christ's Lonely Supremacy

There was one special high-priestly function which was in the mind of the writer to the Hebrews. He thought particularly of the Day of Atonement (Leviticus 16). The Day of Atonement was the greatest day in the Jewish religious year—and still is. While the Temple still stood, it was on that day and on that day alone that atonement was made for *all* sin known and unknown, realized and unrealized. And it was on that day alone that the High Priest entered into the Holy of Holies and sprinkled the blood which made atonement for sin. On no other day could the High Priest enter in, and no one in all the world could enter into the Holy of Holies except him, and him alone (9 : 7, 12). But now that Jesus Christ has come with the perfect sacrifice that yearly sacrifice need never be made again, and—still greater—the way to the inmost presence of God is open, not only to the High Priest but to every man. Atonement is forever made for sin, and the shut door is open for every man.

So then the writer to the Hebrews sets down the lonely supremacy of Jesus Christ. He is greater than the prophets with their partial and temporary and fragmentary message. He is greater than the angels, who are at best only servants. He is greater than Moses, who brought to men the law of God. He is greater than the priests, for He is the perfect priest, who Himself has no sin, and He makes the perfect offering of Himself and His obedience, which never needs to be made again, so that the way to the inmost presence of God is for ever open to every man who believes in Him.

THE NEW AND GREATER PRIESTHOOD

THE SEVENTH CHAPTER of the Letter to the Hebrews is at one and
the same time one of the most difficult and one of the most
fascinating chapters in the New Testament. It is, so far as the
New Testament goes, an almost unique example of Hebrew
exegesis. The writer to the Hebrews wishes to find Old Testament evidence in support of the newness and the supreme
greatness of the priesthood of Jesus Christ. He finds it in the idea
of the priesthood after the order of Melchizedek. He finds an
Old Testament reference to this in Psalm 110 : 4:

> The Lord has sworn
>   and will not change his mind,
> "You are a priest for ever
>   after the order of Melchizedek."

He then goes back to the Genesis story (Genesis 14 : 17-20) for
the one appearance in history of Melchizedek:

> After Abram's return from the defeat of Chedorlaomer and the kings
> who were with him, the king of Sodom went out to meet him at the
> Valley of Shaveh (that is, the King's Valley). And Melchizedek king
> of Salem brought out bread and wine; he was priest of God Most
> High. And he blessed Abram and said:
> "Blessed be Abram by God Most High, maker of heaven and earth;
> and blessed be God Most High, who has delivered your enemies into
> your hand!"
> And Abram gave him a tenth of everything.

Before we go on to look at what the writer to the Hebrews
makes of these passages, we must remember the methods which
Jewish exegesis used. The Jewish scholars paid particular attention
to words, and to the real or the imagined etymology (formation
and origin) of words; they never hesitated to allegorize passages,

and in fact they often argued that the real and the important meaning of a passage was its inner, or spiritual, or allegorical meaning. But what may seem strangest to us is that the Jewish scholars were prepared to base an argument just as much on what Scripture does *not say* as on what Scripture *says*. They were prepared to argue from the silences of Scripture just as much as from the words of Scripture. We shall see all these methods emerging in this chapter in the treatment of these two Old Testament passages about Melchizedek.

The Order of Melchizedek

Let us then see what the writer to the Hebrews extracts from these two passages when he draws the picture of the priesthood of Jesus Christ as the priesthood after the order of Melchizedek.

He begins (7 : 2) by extracting something from the names *Melchizedek* and *Salem*. The name *Melchizedek* itself means *King of Righteousness*; and the name *Salem* is very near *shalōm*, and is taken to mean *peace*. Melchizedek is therefore also *King of Peace*. So we can say at the very beginning that the priesthood after the order of Melchizedek is a royal priesthood, a righteous priesthood, and a peaceful priesthood.

Now (7 : 3 ; 7 : 15-19) the writer to the Hebrews produces his argument from silence, the argument, not from what Scripture says, but from what Scripture does not say. There is no mention of either the birth or the death of Melchizedek; there is no mention of his father or his mother; there is no mention of any time when Melchizedek either became a priest or ceased to be a priest. Now herein is one vast and most significant difference from the Aaronic and the levitical priesthood. An ordinary priest had first and foremost to produce his pedigree. The one qualification without which not even the best man in the world could become a priest was unbroken descent from Aaron, absolutely pure Jewish blood. The first essential was a genealogy, and Melchizedek had none. The argument therefore is that the priesthood of Melchizedek, and therefore the priesthood of Christ, was unique in that they depend, not on any legal enactment not on any matter of genealogy and parentage and descent, but entirely on the personal quality of the priest. The priest himself has in him a quality of life which makes him a priest quite independently of any legal enactment and any genealogical register.

The writer to the Hebrews then produces certain arguments based on the relationship between Melchizedek and Abraham (7 : 4-10). One of them is a very simple argument. Melchizedek blessed Abraham (7 : 7). Now it is obvious that the superior blesses the inferior. We must therefore assume that Melchizedek was greater than even Abraham the father and the founder of the nation and the friend of God. The second argument is more complicated, but would be clear enough to a Jew. Abraham gave tithes to Melchizedek. Now normally the only people who can exact and receive tithes are the Levites, and they receive tithes because it is the law, and they receive them from those who are their flesh and blood brothers. But Melchizedek received tithes from Abraham who was not kin at all to him, and apart altogether from any enactment that such tithes should be paid. He received the tithes entirely as a personal right given to a unique person. More, it is the Levites who *receive* tithes, but in this case it was the Levites who *gave* tithes, for Levi was Abraham's great-grandson, and could be said to be, as it were potentially, in Abraham's body. Therefore, here we have the quite unique situation that Levi, the person who receives tithes, in this case pays them to Melchizedek. Once again the unique superiority of Melchizedek is proved.

Now the writer to the Hebrews switches to another type of argument. The priesthood after the order of Melchizedek is clearly a *new* kind of priesthood (7 : 11), but it is obvious that, if the old priesthood were adequate, no new priesthood would be needed. The very fact that there is a priesthood after the order of Melchizedek is the proof that the levitical priesthood is insufficient and obsolete. But this new priesthood, the priesthood of Jesus Christ after the order of Melchizedek, has even far more radical consequences (7 : 12-14). It was always the law that priests must be of the tribe of *Levi*; Jesus was of the tribe of *Judah*; here is not only a new priesthood, but the end of the old law, for the old law never said anything about a priest from Judah.

Christ's Superior Priesthood

The writer to the Hebrews then goes to Psalm 110 and produces still another argument for the unique superiority of the priesthood after the order of Melchizedek. The Psalmist says: "The Lord has sworn and will not change his mind, 'You are a priest for ever after the order of Melchizedek' " (Psalm 110 : 4). This means that the priesthood after the order of Melchizedek is confirmed by nothing less than the oath of God. No other priesthood was ever thus established and therefore once again the priesthood after the order of Melchizedek is proved to be unique.

Finally (7 : 23-28) the writer to the Hebrews produces two more arguments to prove the superiority of the priesthood of Jesus Christ. The old priests were many, for they came and went as they lived and died. A generation arose and died and had to be replaced; but the priest who is a priest after the order of Melchizedek is *for ever*. He therefore can save to the uttermost and to the end of time. There is an eternal permanence in Him that no earthly priest can ever have.

Finally, the earthly priests, the levitical priests, are sinning and imperfect men, and before they sacrifice for others, they must sacrifice for their own sin. But Jesus is the perfect priest who has no sin and who needs no sacrifice to be offered for Himself. He is not a mere man; he is the Son, appointed by the very oath of God, and in Him the old law and the old cult and the old priesthood are once and for all superseded and overpassed and ended.

So runs the argument that the priesthood of Jesus Christ is the priesthood after the order of Melchizedek and is therefore unique and divine and far superior to the levitical priesthood. It may be that to us it is an argument of little more than antiquarian interest, an argument which we can admire but which does not really satisfy our minds, but to a Jew of the 1st century it must have been an argument both profound and compelling.

8

THE NEW RELATIONSHIP

WE MUST NOW return to the basic idea of the writer to the Hebrews in order that we may see how in still another way he relates Jesus to it. His basic idea is that the search for the soul is for access to reality and access to God, and his basic claim is that it is just that access that Jesus makes possible for men. To illustrate this idea the writer to the Hebrews calls Jesus by two great and vivid titles.

i. He calls him the *archēgos* of salvation and of faith (2 : 10 ; 12 : 2). The translators have given many translations to this word. Captain (A.V.), Pioneer (Moffatt and R.S.V.), Prince Leader or Leader (Weymouth, Kingsley Williams, Phillips, N.E.B.), Author (Twentieth Century New Testament), Source (J. B. Phillips), Beginner (A.V. margin). The word has three main lines of meaning. It can mean *leader* in the sense of commander; it can mean *founder*, the founder of a city, or a philosophy, or a family; it can mean *guide* and *pioneer*.

The Opener of the Way

But there is one flavour which adheres to the word. It almost consistently has the meaning of one who founds something which lasts and into which others can enter, and of someone who opens up a way in which others may follow. Someone has used this analogy. Suppose there is a shipwreck and the only way to rescue is for someone to take a rope and swim ashore with it so that others may follow along the rope that leads to safety, then the one who goes ahead with the rope, at the risk of his life, for others to follow is the *archēgos*.

So then Jesus is the one who blazed the trail, who opened the way, who pioneered the path to reality and to God. He went first for others, for us, to follow.

ii. He calls him the *prodromos*, the forerunner on our behalf (6 : 20). A *prodromos* was always one who went ahead to ensure that it was safe for others to follow. It described the scouts who were sent ahead to see that the way ahead was safe for the main body of the army; it described a ship which went ahead to see that it was safe for the main squadron to sail on. The approach to the harbour in Alexandria in Egypt was difficult and dangerous; the pilot boat therefore sailed in front of a vessel which desired to enter the harbour, and by following the pilot boat the vessel was able to keep in the safe channel. The pilot boat was called the *prodromos*.

Always *prodromos* has this idea of someone going first to make it safe for others to follow. Jesus went first so that it would be safe for us to follow into the presence of God.

So then to the writer to the Hebrews Jesus is the Pioneer who blazes the trail of God, and Jesus is the Forerunner who goes first for others to follow. These are both pictures and ideas which are universal, and which require no explanation because anyone can understand them.

The Covenant Relationship

But the writer to the Hebrews makes great and characteristic use of an idea which is an essential part of Jewish thought, the idea of a *covenant*. A covenant is a relationship entered into between two parties upon certain conditions, and the continuance of the relationship depends upon the maintenance of the conditions. In the religious sense a covenant is a relationship between God and men. But any such relationship between God and men has certain distinguishing characteristics, and these characteristics are indicated and underlined in the word that the Biblical writers use for *covenant*. The ordinary Greek word for a *covenant* is *sunthēkē*, but *sunthēkē* describes a treaty, a bargain, an agreement, a relationship into which the two parties enter on equal terms;

75

they can mutually discuss the terms of it; each can try to lay down his own conditions; they meet on an equal level. Now this is clearly not the case in any relationship between God and man. Man is not, and cannot ever be, on equal terms with God. In any relationship between man and God it is God who alone can take the initiative, and man can only accept or refuse both the offer and the conditions of God; man cannot argue and bargain with God, as he can with other men. Therefore, the word that the Bible uses for a covenant is *diathēkē*, and for this reason— *diathēkē* in ordinary Greek is the regular word for a *will*, which is the one kind of human agreement in which one party gives and in which the other party can do no more than take, and take on the terms laid down. So then the Biblical word for *covenant* is *diathēkē* in order to stress the fact that in a covenant the whole initiative lies with God, and man cannot argue and bargain; he can only accept—or refuse—the offer and its terms.

Now the covenant idea is basic to the whole Jewish conception of religion. Israel is the nation which is uniquely in a covenant relationship with God. We see that covenant relationship being entered into in Exodus 24 : 3-8. The great covenant between God and Israel had its beginning immediately after the giving of the law to Moses. The law was the condition of the covenant. Burnt offerings are sacrificed; half of the blood is thrown on the altar; the book of the law is read to the people, and they pledge themselves to be obedient to it; then the people themselves are sprinkled with the blood of the covenant; and the relationship is initiated.

Now here are the basic ideas. God has approached Israel to be His people; the condition of that relationship is obedience to the law; sacrifice is made; and the covenant is ratified in blood. Here then is the old covenant and it is based on sacrifice and on obedience to the law.

But then another basic idea enters into the relationship. The covenant is dependent on obedience to the law. No man and no nation can perfectly keep the law. There are therefore breaches of the law, and when the law is broken the relationship is broken. It is to mend that relationship that the whole hierarchy of the priesthood and the whole apparatus of sacrifice is designed. The law is broken; the relationship should also be broken; but sacrifice is made; and the sacrifice combined with penitence and contrition is meant to restore the lost relationship.

Everything seems to be provided for, but there enters into the matter the one inescapable flaw. The sacrifice and the blood of animals can never restore the lost relationship (9 : 1-10). The institution of the priesthood and the ritual of animal sacrifice is quite inadequate to cleanse the conscience and to restore and maintain the relationship between man and God. In a word the old covenant has failed in that which it was meant to do and to maintain.

Now, as the writer to the Hebrews sees it, Scripture had actually foreseen this, and had provided for it. For Scripture speaks about a *new* covenant, and if there is a new covenant, then clearly the old covenant is already obsolete (8 : 13). That new covenant is the covenant which Jeremiah speaks about (Hebrews 8 : 8-12 ; Jeremiah 31 : 31-34). That new covenant has two salient characteristics:

> This is the covenant that I will make with them, after these days, says the Lord: I will put my laws on their hearts, and write them on their minds,

and,

> I will remember their sin and their misdeeds no more
> (Jeremiah 31 : 33, 34 ; Hebrews 10 : 16, 17).

Two things stand out about this promise. The new covenant is not a thing of external controls and pressures and laws; it is written on the heart. It comes not from the externally applied discipline of the law, but from the inner compulsion of the recreated heart. And—still more of a radical change and still more astonishing—there is in it *no mention of sacrifice at all*.

It is, as the writer to the Hebrews sees it, this new covenant which Jesus Christ has initiated and brought about, this quite new relationship with God. And He can do so because He is the perfect priest, and He has brought the perfect offering, which renders all other offerings superfluous and unnecessary. The covenant needs its blood and its sacrifice, for everything is purified with blood, and without the shedding of blood there is no forgiveness of sins (9 : 22). But with His blood He has brought in the new covenant and with His sacrifice He has offered a sacrifice which needs no repetition for ever.

Jesus—The Mediator

This conception of Jesus as the one in whom the new covenant becomes effective, the one who creates the new relationship between God and man, leads the writer to the Hebrews to apply two other titles to Jesus, which are specially connected with this area of thought.

First, he calls Jesus the *mediator of the new and the better* covenant (9 : 15 ; 12 : 24). The Greek for *mediator* is *mesitēs*. *Mesos* means *in the middle*, and a *mesitēs* is one who stands in the middle between two parties who are estranged so that by his reconciling work he can bring them together again. Jesus is the middleman between men and God; He brings men to God and He brings God to men in His own person. By standing in the middle He brings about the new relationship between men and God.

Second, He is the *surety* of the better covenant (7 : 22). The word is *egguos*, and it means the *sponsor* or the *guarantor*. To have a relationship with God in which there is no need of any sacrifice, in which the way to God is wide open, in which any man can draw near, is so great and so glorious that we might think that it is too good to be true. But Jesus is the guarantor of the blessed reality of this new relationship with God.

In regard to the connection of Jesus with the new covenant the writer to the Hebrews uses an argument which may seem very strange to the modern mind. The Alexandrian scholars loved subtle arguments, and in particular they liked arguments which depended on the use of words. They frequently founded an argument on two meanings of the same word. The writer to the Hebrews does that in 9 : 15-17. It will be remembered that we have already seen that the word *diathēkē* is used by the writer to the Hebrews in the sense of *covenant*, although its regular meaning in secular Greek is *will*.

In 9 : 15 the writer to the Hebrews speaks of Jesus as the mediator of a new *covenant*. But in 9 : 17 he makes the point that a *will* can only come into force in consequence of a death. In both verses the word is the same, in both verses it is *diathēkē*. The writer is, as it were, punning on its meaning. Jesus is the mediator of the new *covenant* (*diathēkē*) but a *will* (*diathēkē*) cannot come into force without a death, and so to make the new covenant effective Jesus had to die. Thus by this method, a method which, however strange to us, would have been a sound argument to the reader of his own day, the writer to the Hebrews finds an argument to prove that it cost the death of Jesus Christ to establish the new covenant, the new relationship, between God and man.

It may be that there are times in this area of his thought when the writer to the Hebrews is moving in a world which is strange to us, but the one great simple fact remains that to speak of Jesus and the new covenant is quite simply to say that through Jesus Christ there is open to every man who will receive it a new relationship with God.

9

WORDS OF WARNING

THE WRITER TO the Hebrews has a characteristic method of writing. He does not normally intermingle exposition with warning and exhortation; he rather alternates them. He has passages of exposition followed by passages of threat and appeal, and it has been well said that his passages of direct warning are as stern as anything in the New Testament. It is at these words of warning that we must now look. We cannot include them all in so brief a survey as this, but we can look at the most important of them.

i. The first of them comes in 2 : 1-5, and it is a warning against *the danger of drifting*. It would be fatally easy for the Christian to drift away, and so, like a careless mariner, to miss the haven and to end in shipwreck on the rocks.

For the Christian, as the writer to the Hebrews sees it, this is doubly inexcusable. The Jews have the Law, and the Law was given by angels. In the Law each transgression has its prescribed punishment. No one can break the Law with impunity. If that is true of the Law, how much truer it must be of the Christian message.

Characteristics of the Message

So the writer to the Hebrews picks out three characteristics of the Christian message as it has come to his readers. First, it was brought by none other than the Lord Himself. Second, it was attested and confirmed to them by the words and the witness of those who were actual hearers of the Lord and eye-witnesses of the salvation events. Third, its uniqueness is guaranteed by the amazing powers and gifts of the Spirit, manifested in miraculous events, within the Christian community.

The greater the revelation, the greater the responsibility; and if men are condemned for neglecting the older revelation, how can they escape condemnation if they refuse the still greater revelation in Jesus Christ? "How shall we escape, if we neglect such a great salvation?" (2 : 3).

ii. The second passage is a long passage and comes in 3 : 7-4 : 13. The exposition is largely based on Psalm 95 : 7-11. Because of their rebellion and their disobedience the children of Israel who left Egypt for the desert journey never entered into their rest. The Psalmist appeals to his hearers to-day to hear God's voice and to-day not to harden their hearts as their forefathers did.

The argument of the writer to the Hebrews, although it stretches out to some length in his exposition of it, can be very briefly summarized. It was their rebellious disobedience which kept the Israelites from entering into and enjoying the promised rest. But for all that, even if they never entered into it, the rest remains, for God rested on the seventh day after His works (Genesis 2 : 2 ; Hebrews 4 : 4). And yet in spite of it the Psalmist appeals to his people *to-day* to hear and to answer the invitation of God. And so the writer to the Hebrews urges his readers in obedience and in fidelity to seek that rest *to-day*. It will not always be to-day; the opportunity is now, but the opportunity will pass. Let them, *now*, *to-day*, in obedient faith enter into the rest that God has promised them, the rest that their forefathers missed and never enjoyed. Here the writer to the Hebrews is insisting that: "Now is the time." He is beseeching them to avoid the tragedy of the lost opportunity.

iii. The third exhortation is one which occurs more than once, and it may be said to be the supreme theological and practical problem of the Letter to the Hebrews, for in this Letter there is a series of passages which seem on the face of it to say that there comes a time when both repentance and forgiveness are impossible. The passages in question are 6 : 1-8; 10 : 26-31, and 12 : 16, 17. These passages are of such importance and of such difficulty that we must set them down in full.

For it is impossible to restore again to repentance those who have once been enlightened, who have tasted the heavenly gift, and have become partakers of the Holy Spirit, and have tasted the goodness of the word of God and the powers of the age to come, if they then commit apostasy, since they crucify the Son of God on their own account and hold him up to contempt (6 : 4-6).

For if we sin deliberately after receiving the knowledge of the truth, there no longer remains a sacrifice for sins, but a fearful prospect of judgment, and a fury of fire which will consume the adversaries (10 : 26, 27).

See to it . . . that no one be immoral or irreligious like Esau, who sold his birthright for a single meal. For you know that afterward, when he desired to inherit the blessing, he was rejected, for he found no chance to repent, though he sought it with tears (12 : 16, 17).

It is the first passage which has the basis of the matter in it. It seems on the face of it to mean that a man can reach a stage when there is no forgiveness possible for him. The matter could even be narrowed. The word *enlightened* is from the Greek verb *phōtizein*, which did come at least in later times to be regularly and almost technically connected with *baptism*. And therefore this has been taken that there can be no forgiveness for post-baptismal sin. We need not enter into the argument as to whether it is post-baptismal sin which is in question. The real problem is the conception of a stage when a man has been enlightened and yet he can still reach a stage when he is beyond forgiveness.

The problem about this is twofold. It seems to run counter to the teaching of the Gospel and of the other New Testament Letters; and it seems to collide violently with the doctrine of the indefectibility of grace, and the belief that a man cannot fall from grace. When Cromwell was dying he asked about this doctrine of grace and he was assured that a man cannot fall from grace. "Then I am happy," he said, "for I am sure that I was once in a state of grace." Certainly this is a terrible passage, "charged," as Moffatt put it, "with austerity." Let us then see what various New Testament expositors have made of it. Let us begin by looking at what we may not unfairly call evasions of its full meaning.

(a) It is suggested that the word *impossible* (*adunaton*) should be taken rather in the sense of *supremely difficult*. One Latin manuscript (d) actually has *difficile* instead of *impossibile*. Or, it has been suggested, the meaning is that it is impossible by way of the Law of Moses, but not impossible by way of the grace of God. These attempts to water down the meaning of *adunaton* are not really justified.

(b) Calvin stressed the word *tasted*. He felt that the passage is speaking of those who have *tasted* the heavenly gift, and *tasted* the goodness of the word of God (6 : 4, 5), and that the word *tasted* is, as it were, opposed to a word such as *swallowed*. He then held that the passage refers to those who did not really inwardly know and experience the grace of God, those who had merely an inkling of it, those who were irradiated by only some sparks of the life in Christ. This certainly will not do, because in 2 : 9 the writer to the Hebrews speaks of Jesus Christ *tasting* death, and he cannot by that mean that Jesus did not really and truly experience death. These expressions must go back to Psalm 34 : 8:

O taste and see that the Lord is good!
Happy is the man who takes refuge in him!

And in a passage like that the word *to taste* clearly means to experience to the full.

Methods of Interpretation

It can be seen that the evasions do not really offer any way out.

(c) We may now look at a method of interpretation which many expositors, of whom Farrar is typical, have adopted, and which is based on a careful stressing of the tenses in the passage.

If they then commit apostasy is in the Greek one word. It is an aorist participle, *parapesontas*. Since the aorist normally indicates one completed act in past time, this could simply mean, *when they have committed a sin*. In the Greek *they crucify* is also a participle (*anastaurountas*) and in this case it is a *present* participle which indicates continuous action, and ought to mean, *if they continue to crucify the Son of God*. Now, still further, *to restore*

83

again is in the Greek a present infinitive (*anakainizein*) and could perfectly correctly and even naturally mean *to go on restoring*. The sense would then be something like this: "Once a man has been enlightened, and tasted the grace of God, if he has committed some sin, it is impossible to go on restoring him, if he persists in crucifying Christ again, or, while he continues to crucify Christ again." The point would then be that it is impossible to go on restoring a man who has been enlightened and who then not only commits one act of sin and apostasy, but who goes on continuously and persistently re-crucifying Christ with his conduct. The condemnation would then be of *persistent* sin. So long as a man quite unrepentantly persists in his sin, he cannot be restored. But let him stop persisting, and let him repent, and then forgiveness is still open to him.

This interpretation stresses the *persistence*. It is equally possible to start with the same general view of the passage, but to stress not so much the continuousness and the persistence of the sinning, as the *deliberate* nature of the sin. This is the view of James Moffatt who holds that the man who is so unsparingly condemned is the *deliberate* apostate, the man who *deliberately* abandons the Christian confession, the man who recreates within himself that very same attitude of mind and heart which was responsible for the crucifixion of Jesus.

Whether we take continuousness or deliberation to be the essence of the matter, the result of this is that the forgiveness is necessarily withheld *so long as the man continues in this state*, but if the man repents and mends his ways then forgiveness is still open to him.

There is no doubt that this is an attractive view, and there may well be no hesitation in accepting this as the fully Christian position, but it must remain doubtful if this is what the writer to the Hebrews really meant. There are two further views which may well have in them the essence of the matter.

(d) First, there is the view also put forward by James Moffatt that this is an instance of *a man speaking in a missionary situation*. "To our author the unpardonable sin is apostasy, and his view is that of a missionary." Modern parallels can be quoted in which in

84

a missionary situation even quite grave and serious moral faults will be pardoned, "but if a Christian should again sacrifice to his ancestors or have anything to do with magic, no earnest Christian will speak in his favour; he is regarded as one who has fallen back into heathenism, and therefore as lost." It may simply be that the violence of the reaction of the writer to the Hebrews against apostasy is simply due to the situation in which he finds himself, for the one thing which could undermine and discredit the position of the growing Church, set like an island in a sea of paganism, was the apostasy of its members. This then will not be meant to be a universal pronouncement, but a warning for the actual situation of the readers of the Letter.

(e) Second, and lastly, there is the view of A. B. Bruce. Bruce wrote: "The Bible is an excellent book for the purpose of practical religion, but rather a tantalizing book for the systematic theologian. Its writers know nothing of the caution of the system-maker, but express themselves in strong, unqualified terms, which are the torment of the dogmatist and the despair of the controversialist. The author of this Epistle in particular writes not as a theorist, but as an observer of facts." This is undoubtedly true, and it really means that in these passages the writer to the Hebrews was not thinking of laying down a universal law. With all the passion of a preacher and with all the vividness of an orator and with all the deep concern of a pastor and with the anxiety of a missionary, not only for his flock, but also for the whole Church, he writes for the immediate situation, a situation in which apostasy was the supreme danger.

Warnings of Danger

iv. There remain three other passages of warning and exhortation at which we may look, but we can look at them much more quickly, for they are straightforward warnings of danger, and it is true to say that basically and essentially they all contemplate the same danger.

(a) The first is in 5 : 11-14. The complaint of the writer to the Hebrews here is that he is afraid that his people are not able to take the teaching that he wishes to give them. They should be adult and mature Christians, ready for the strong meat of advanced teaching, but in point of fact they are still no better than children, who can digest no more than milk.

This is a warning to the Christian who will not grow up. This is the condemnation of the man who still has, not a childlike, but a childish faith. Christian faith must necessarily be a growth and a development. The experiences of life are bound to make a man discover more and more of the greatness of the faith which he holds. God is infinite in goodness and in truth, and a lifetime cannot be enough to discover His unsearchable riches. There is therefore something wrong with the man for whom his faith is a static and not a growing and a developing experience.

Someone has said that normally, especially in the case of the student, there will be three stages in faith. There will be the *un-critical* stage, in which at the beginning there is an experience of Jesus Christ which is so direct and compelling that the questions have not yet begun to arise. There is the *critical* stage. Most people pass through a stage of faith when they have more questions than they can answer, a stage in which they come to see that the so-called simple faith is not so simple as they thought, and that there are inevitable questions to be asked and inevitable problems to be solved. And finally there is the *post-critical* stage, when a man emerges with a faith tried and tested, all the stronger because it faced the questions, all the stronger because it refused to evade the problems, all the stronger because it passed through its doubts.

The writer to the Hebrews is afraid for Christians who are so spiritually lazy that they will not think, for the man who will not think, will never grow up, and maturity in faith is needed as much as maturity in any other sphere.

(b) The second of these passages is in 10 : 35-39. The appeal of this passage is that the readers, through lack of endurance, should not throw away the fine record that they have already achieved. If it is the case that the recipients of the Letter were priests who had become Christians, they had given up much both in regard to prestige and emoluments. From this passage with its quotation of Habakkuk 2 : 3, 4, with its promise that the coming one will not delay, we may well assume that these converts had expected the Second Coming very soon, and were disappointed that it had not happened, for it seemed that their sacrifice was to bring them nothing. The writer urges upon them the duty of *endurance*. The word is *hupomonē*, an almost untranslatable word (see p. 38). Frequently the Authorized Version translates it *patience*, but it means far more than patience. It means that attitude of mind which can accept the chances and the changes, the sorrows and the tears, the disappointments and delays of life and in accepting them change them into glory. It does not mean simply a passive sitting down and letting the experiences of life flow over one; it means the ability to transmute every experience into something of shining value.

So this is the exhortation to learn to wait and never to lose the glory.

(c) The third of these passages is in 12 : 1-17. It is a passage which indicates that the readers of the Letter are going through trials and difficulties in their Christian life. It urges them to do two things. First, it urges them to look at Jesus, who because He endured the cross and the shame entered into His glory. Neither for Him nor for His followers could there be a crown without a cross. Second, it urges them to remember that all chastisement and all discipline are in essence a privilege and compliment. They are a sign of love. It would be a poor parent who never disciplined his child, and even so it is those whom God loves whom God chastens. If there were no chastening it would be a sign of God's abandonment of them. The chastening and the discipline are the sign of the interest and the confidence and the love of God.

All the warnings are warnings to hold on to faith and hope when the experiences of life are trying to take them away.

10

FAITH AND LIFE

AT FIRST SIGHT it might well seem that the Letter to the Hebrews is an otherworldly book. Its theme is access to God and access to reality. It thinks in terms of entering into the presence of God, and of entering into that invisible and unseen world of ideas in which reality lies. It might well be thought that anyone who started out from such ideas as these would be much more concerned with theological and philosophical abstractions than with practical things, but the fact is that no writer in the New Testament has a more practical mind than the writer to the Hebrews.

We may see this in its most fundamental form in his conception of faith. Faith, he says, is the assurance of things hoped for, the conviction of things not seen (11 : 1). That is to say, quite simply, faith is the certainty that hopes will come true, and faith is the conviction that the unseen and invisible realities not only exist, but are the most important things of all.

Faith—an Intellectual Conviction

The eleventh chapter of the Letter to the Hebrews is the honour roll of faith, and when we study it, and when we look at the examples of faith which he chooses, we can see what faith meant to him.

i. For him faith begins with what we might almost call an intellectual conviction. Faith begins with the conviction that God is, and that He rewards those who seek Him (11 : 6). The two halves of this basis of belief are very different. It has never been difficult to persuade the vast majority of men that God exists. In this world we see an ordered unity. Suns rise and set; tides ebb and flow; seasons come and go in their ordered cycle; the solar system with the sun and the stars and the planets is a vast ordered machine which never goes wrong; the same action is always followed by the same reaction. It is impossible to deny the order of the world, and where there is order, there must be mind. As it has been said, no astronomer can be an atheist, although that has not proved universally true. But the argument from order to a mind which begat and maintains the order is strong.

With this first half of the claim of the writer to the Hebrews most thinking men would agree, for it is not difficult to persuade people to admit the existence of God. But the second half of his proposition, the claim that God rewards those who seek Him, is another matter, for this basically assumes that God is interested in men, that He cares what they do, that their reaction to Him matters to Him. To many, as we have already seen, this is the very opposite of what we would naturally believe about God, for, it is claimed, if God is interested in men, if God cares for men, if, to put it at its height, God loves men, then the detached serenity of God is gone, and God is involved in the affairs of men. This men have always found it very hard to believe, and yet this is precisely the meaning of Jesus Christ and of the fact of His incarnation. Nevertheless, for the writer to the Hebrews the twin foundation pillars of faith are the conviction that God is and that God cares.

Faith in Life

We must next ask how this faith manifests itself in a man's life.

ii. It manifests itself in a certain attitude to life. It manifests itself in the conviction that we are strangers and pilgrims here, that here we have no abiding city, that we are seeking our real homeland, that city whose maker and builder is God (11 : 13-16). In this attitude everything is seen in the light of eternity. In it the supreme thing about life is that it has got a beyond. So far from rendering this life unimportant, this belief clothes life with a new significance, for it means that life is on the way to somewhere, and that there is still a world in which promises will come true, even if we have to leave this world with them still unrealized. Robert Louis Stevenson tells of a byreman who was asked if he never got completely weary of working day in and day out with the cattle and with the filth of the byre. "He that has something ayont need never weary," he answered. He who has a beyond to his world will never weary. Faith is the attitude of life which never loses the awareness of the beyond.

iii. Faith manifests itself in total obedience to God. That obedience may be such that it makes a man look like a fool as it did in the case of Noah (11 : 7), building his incredible ark. It may be such that it demands that a man should be prepared to give up even his most precious possessions and relationships for the sake of God as in the case of Abraham and Isaac (11 : 24-28). The inner faith becomes the outward obedience which will go to any length in accepting, and translating into action, the will of God.

iv. This faith will manifest itself in the willingness to make the even reckless venture in answer to the challenge of God. Faith answers the summons: "Go out!" So Abraham went out not knowing where he was going, only knowing that he must go (11 : 8, 15). So Moses preferred identification in adventure with his own people to safety and security at the court of Pharaoh (11 : 24-28). So the people who dared the crossing of the Red Sea and shared in the destruction of Jericho were prepared to go forward with God (11 : 29, 30). In one of his moments of danger John Bunyan fought down the fears of which he was ashamed and said, as he thought of climbing the ladder to the scaffold: "I will leap off the ladder even blindfold into eternity. Lord Jesus, if thou wilt catch me, do. If not, *I will venture for thy name*." Faith manifests itself in the willingness to venture for the name of God.

v. This faith manifests itself in the belief of the possibility of the impossible. Against all the possibilities Sarah believed that God could give her a child and He did (11 : 11). This faith has banished the word impossible from its vocabulary and from its mind.

vi. This faith manifests itself in the belief of the power and the will of God to bless. Thus Isaac and Jacob bless their children in the certainty that God can make the blessing into fact (11 : 20, 21). It is the conviction that God's arm will never be shortened and His power will never grow less.

vii. This faith manifests itself in the willingness to throw in our lot with the people of God, even when it seems that the big battalions are on the other side. So Rahab takes the side of the people of God even when they seem to have little chance (11 : 31). Faith is the conviction that the ultimate victory is with God.

viii. This faith manifests itself in the heroism of the human spirit, whether that heroism be the heroism which wins the famous victory or the heriosm that can bear defeat and perse-cution and death (11 : 32-38). Faith is the dynamic which gives men power to dare, to do, and to endure, to pass the breaking-point and not to break.

Faith manifests itself in life, and the New Testament writers did not forget the indissoluble connection between theology and ethics. The writer to the Hebrews is no exception, and in chapters 12 and 13 he urges their ethical duties upon his readers.

He urges them to live in peace with all (12 : 14). The word for peace is *shalōm* in Hebrew, and one of its great meanings is right relationships between man and man. The Christian ethic is an ethic of personal relationships, and a man cannot be in a right relationship with God so long as he is in a wrong relationship with his fellow men. He reminds them of their family duties. Marriage is to be held in honour; they are not to be led away by the false asceticism which belittles marriage; and the marriage bond is to be observed with all fidelity (13 : 4).

Life in the Church

He has advice for them within the Church and the brother-hood. They are to live in brotherly love (13 : 1); they are never to forget the Christian duty of kindness and of sharing with one another (13 : 16); they are to remember the duty of hospitality (13 : 2). In a pagan society it was a great thing—and it still is—that Christian homes should always be open to welcome Christians who are strangers in strange places. They are to remember the faith and the heroism of their past leaders, and they are to give to their present leaders obedience and respect (13 : 7, 17). Within the Christian society they are to keep the faith clean, and pure, and unsullied. They are to see that no root of bitterness (Deuteronomy 29 : 18), that is, no invitation to apostasy, enters in (12 : 15), and they are not to be led away by misguided and misguiding teachers (13 : 9).

In their own lives they are to be neither immoral nor irreligious (12 : 16, 17). They are not to be like Esau who flung away his birthright for a meal. They are not to be people who cannot see beyond material things.

They are to remember all who are in prison and in any kind of trouble (13 : 3). Every Christian should feel a personal responsibility for every other Christian who is in any kind of need. They are not to love money overmuch. Why should they? They have something that is precious beyond all money values; they have the promise that God will never leave them nor forsake them. Their security comes not from the possession of money, but from the possession of the promise and the presence of God (13 : 5 ; Deuteronomy 31 : 6, 8 ; Joshua 1 : 5 ; Psalm 118 : 6).

Of course, all this is going to be difficult, and of course, all this is going to lead them into trouble. But there are two things which they must remember. They are called out of the world. Jesus Christ was crucified outside the city wall, for the sacrifice for sin was in fact burned outside the camp (Leviticus 16 : 27). They too must separate themselves and go out (13 : 13). And further, they are in the very nature of things people who have no abiding city in the world, but whose eyes are fixed on the beyond (13 : 14). They are to live in the eternal Christian paradox, the paradox of involvement and of separation. In one sense, no one is so involved in the sin and the suffering and the sorrow of the world as the Christian; and in another sense, no one is so detached from the world as the Christian. He is the servant and the lover of all men, and yet his citizenship is in heaven. And it is the very fact that he lives in the shadow of eternity that makes him the servant of all in the world of time.

PERMANENT VALUES

WE MUST BRING our study of the Letter to the Hebrews to a close by asking what permanent contribution it makes to religious thought. Any book is necessarily written in the language, the pictures, the thought forms of its own time; but any book has certain underlying conceptions and ideas which are expressed in these temporary forms. What then are the permanent ideas of the Letter to the Hebrews which are just as relevant for us as for those who first read it?

Access to God

i. The writer to the Hebrews had a basic conception of religion which is permanently valid. For him religion is access to God. Oddly enough, he would well have understood what we meant, if we put this in a perfectly modern way and said that religion means knowledge of and access to ultimate reality, for he knew all about the invisible eternal forms, ideas and patterns of which the things of time are only imperfect transient copies.

And yet, if we put it this way, if we say that religion is access to God and access to ultimate reality, it sounds all very abstract and theological and philosophical. We may put it much more simply. Religion for the writer to the Hebrews is being in a right relationship to God. It is knowing God as an intimate friend rather than as the distant stranger, whom we can never know, or the stern judge, of whom we must ever be in fear. We can put it even more simply yet. Religion is the realization that, sinners as we are, we are admitted to the friendship of God

The Work of Christ

ii. The writer is perfectly sure that this relationship is only possible because of what Jesus Christ is and did.

It has been well noted that the Letter to the Hebrews, although it is a comparatively short book, has one of the completest Christologies in the New Testament. It implies the *pre-existence* of the Son, for it was through Him that the world was created (1 : 2). It states the *incarnation* of the Son, for there was a time when He was made a little lower than the angels (2 : 9). It stresses *the earthly life* of the Son, in which He went through the agony of Gethsemane, and in which He knew all the temptations to which the human life is heir (5 : 8 ; 4 : 15). All through it there is the memory of the *Cross*, the sacrifice made by the Son for men (12 : 2). Equally, the writer to the Hebrews stresses the *Ascension* and the present glory of the Son; and the Ascension implies the Resurrection (2 : 9 ; 10 : 12 ; 12 : 2). For him Jesus Christ was not a dead hero, however great in the memory, He was the living, reigning Lord. And, finally, he stresses the *Second Coming*, of which, as he sees it, the Christian must never give up the hope (9 : 28 ; 10 : 37). The writer to the Hebrews never loses sight of the centrality of Jesus—and of His total adequacy for time and for eternity.

It is this Jesus who establishes and makes possible the new relationship between man and God. It is true that in working out this conception the writer to the Hebrews uses pictures and conceptions which were relevant for his own age rather than for ours. He uses the idea of a *covenant*, a relationship between man and God, offered solely by the initiative of God, and dependent on man's keeping the conditions of it. He uses the idea of Jesus as *High Priest*, the *pontifex*, literally the *bridge-builder*, between man and God.

However we interpret the fact, the fact remains that it was the life and the death and the resurrection of Jesus Christ which made possible the new relationship between God and man. Quite certainly, without Him that relationship would not have been possible, for without Him we would never have known that God desired it, and never have known what God is like.

The Seven Dangers

Here then are the two great conceptions of the Letter to the

Hebrews. Religion is basically man entering into friendship with God on the initiative of God, and that friendship is only possible through the work and the person of Jesus Christ.

But, as we noted before, the mind of the writer to the Hebrews is intensely practical, and because of that one of the most permanently valuable of the features of his Letter is his intense awareness of the dangers and the threats to true religion.

i. There is the danger of *drift instead of decision* (2 : 1). It is possible for the non-Christian to drift through life, uncommitted to anything and to anyone. The Christian is a man who has made a decision, and whose life and whose every action are dominated by that decision. He knows where he is going, and his life is dictated by the determination to get there.

ii. There is the danger of *weariness instead of endurance* (10 : 35-38 ; 12 : 12, 13). There is the ever-present danger of growing weary of waiting, tired of struggling. Christianity never offered any man an easy way. It is he who endures to the end who will be saved (Matthew 10 : 22 ; 24 : 13). There may be many more glamorous and romantic qualities than simple perseverance, but there is none more necessary and none more valuable. The world is full of people who began things and never finished them. The Christian life is an uphill road, but he who travels it may be sustained by the continual consciousness of the companion of his way and the goal at the end.

iii. There is the danger of *stagnation instead of progress* (5 : 11-6 : 1). Nothing has done the Church more harm than the way in which it has so often refused the adventure of thought and the challenge to action. There would seem to be in religion an almost instinctive fear of that which is new. There has been so often in the Church a kind of inborn and inbuilt resistance to change. We should not speak of change *and* decay, but change *or* decay. The Christian should be a man stripped for mental and social action, not a man whose one desire is to keep things as they are.

iv. There is the danger of the search for *comfort instead of discipline* (12 : 4-11). It may well be that this has come from the presentation of Christianity as something which brings rest and peace and joy in the wrong sense of the term. It is when a man becomes a Christian that the fight begins, for then he is presented with a set of standards and attainments of which he never dreamed before. True, there is a deep and an abiding peace, but it is the peace which comes, not from evading issues, but from facing them, which knows that chastisement is a part of love.

v. There is the danger of *isolation instead of fellowship*. There is one very significant phrase in the Letter to the Hebrews—"not neglecting to meet together as is the habit of some" (10 : 25). To fall away from the fellowship of worship is the first step to falling away from the fellowship of faith. It is in the fellowship of worship that a man finds his fellow men and God. Christianity in isolation is seldom—perhaps never—a practical proposition.

vi. There is the danger of *apostasy instead of loyalty* (6 : 1-8). Loyalty has never been an easy thing. It has never been easy not to be ashamed of the Gospel of Jesus Christ; it has never been easy to take the stand which means being different, for no man likes to stand alone. But to the intense seriousness of the writer to the Hebrews the apostate is the most serious sinner of all, for by his deliberate apostasy he becomes a sharer in the crucifixion of Jesus Christ. The writer to the Hebrews is not thinking of that disloyalty into which a man may be swept by the impulse or the passion, the terror or the fear, of an unguarded moment, he is thinking of the quite deliberate abandonment of Jesus Christ by the man who knows what he is doing. Than this the writer to the Hebrews can see no more terrible sin.

vii. There is one more danger for which we do not need to quote any particular passage, for it runs through the whole letter. It is the danger of *looking in the wrong direction*. The Christian may look *forward* to the hope that is set before him; he may look *upward* to the Jesus who is the pioneer and perfecter of his faith; but he may not look *backward*. So long as his thoughts linger longingly on the old ways and the past things he has not made the clear cut decision. As the writer to the Hebrews sees it, the Christian is a man who looks up and who goes on.